AF244213

Journey for a Tomorrow

Victor H. Anderson
Founder of the Feri Tradition

Cornelia Benavidez takes takes the reader on a voyage of discovery, both inner and outer, through the earthly paradise that is Hawaii. There is magic and mystery, poetry and prophecy, wit and wildness to be seen and heard within these pages. And ultimately, a message of hope for us and for all who dwell on our beautiful planet. – L.Shimmer

Journey for a Tomorrow

Cornelia Benavidez

Megalithica Books
Stafford England

Journey for a Tomorrow
by Cornelia Benavidez
© 2019 First edition

All rights reserved, including the right to reproduce this book, or portions thereof, in any form.

The rights of Cornelia Benavidez to be identified as the author of this work have been asserted by her in accordance with the Copyright, Designs and Patents Act, 1988.

Editor: Louise Coquio
Layout: Storm Constantine
Cover Design: Peter Hollinghurst

All photos are from the author's personal collection and were taken by her or Linda unless otherwise stated in the text that they derive from Wiki-commons common use

ISBN: 978-1-912241-12-5
MB0204

Set in Book Antiqua

A Megalithica Books Publication
An imprint of Immanion Press
info@immanion-press.com
http://www.immanion-press.com

Contents

Prayer to Lono

E kala e Lono
kala ia na kala o ke alii Kane
e kala i ka kala o ke alii kane
e kala i ka ke alii Wahine
E kala i ka kala o na Kahuna
E kala i ka kala o ka hu ka maa ai nana
He pule kala keia ia oe, Lono

Forgive O Lono
pardon all the sins of the chiefs
pardon the sins of the men chiefs
pardon the sins of the chiefesses
Pardon the sins of the priests
Pardon the sins of the citizens of the land
whatever you see
This is a petition to you for forgiveness, Lono

Introduction

It has been 33 years since my Journey. The story about the adventure and quest, 'Journey for a Tomorrow', originally 'A Journey for Victor,' was started not long after my epic trip to Hawaii with my friend Linda back in 1986, but my recounting of those adventures was put aside when earthquakes, moves and various challenges and opportunities filled my days. As time went by, there was also the growing needs of Victor and Cora as they grew older (my friends and teachers in the Feri Tradition which, as Victor and Cora taught it, is an orally passed down tradition founded by them in California in the 1960s, although Victor had been practicing Feri and various other pagan teachings since a child). I had my notes and had started Journey before Victor passed so he did get to see the first chapters, but I did not get the chance to finish the story until I wrote it as a series for a small local Feri magazine called 'Witcheye'. This was mostly distributed to Victor's initiates, students and friends after his passing in 2001. Cora was so happy that I had completed Journey and enjoyed me reading the manuscript to her at her bedside.

The purpose of this book is not only to share that story with a wider audience but also to introduce more of the thoughts and philosophy that Victor held so dear. It is now the time to share clearly the deeper meaning of the mystery and quest Linda and I were called to.

Of course, some may still wonder why I waited so long to write it all in book form. There were several good reasons for this. Number one, perhaps, was at the time there was so much going on in the metaphysical, New Age, and the old and new pagan traditions here in the America, and it was not till many years later that I came to fully understand that much was also transpiring around the world at that time, especially in the United Kingdom. There were so many books and speakers talking about their various religious and transcendental experiences. For some it seemed like an honest attempt to share their experience to encourage others to follow suit. For others it was a way to share feelings of love and peace, a forerunner of what can await us beyond the veil of death, and what we can and should strive for here in life. The kids of the Love and Peace generation were coming out in force in politics, music and all the creative arts, while long-established stars were becoming more vocal about their political and even spiritual experiences. It was the time of Shirley MacLaine's (an award-winning actress from the 50's to present day) book '*Out on a Limb,*' which shocked the people of her generation, for it featured her fearless exploration of the metaphysical and spiritual worlds. It seemed to give a thumbs up to the younger generations to step up and have the guts to look within and about themselves to find what really gives one's life joy and meaning. For a while, especially where I was in the San Francisco Bay area in California, people's hearts filled with hope after the tumultuous years from 1978 to 1986. There were more books than ever, with movies spreading self-help movements, with the rise of Scientology, EST, and gurus from India all offering a new perspective or the use of a new set of psychological or philosophical wares.

The old religions and paths from all over the world were rising up to be heard. On one hand, it was an exciting time, a chance to finally dig in, either figuratively or literally, as boundaries were crossed, and new discoveries made. Voices rose, calling to question humankind's interpretations of history and archeological finds. The desire for 'truth', and connection to something bigger than our capricious, narcissistic nonsense, was in our silent prayers and on the lips of so many.

So, it was only natural when I returned from my adventure, at first, to want to write it all down. To sing from the rooftops and tell everyone what had happened. Especially the people at Amron, my Metaphysical Church, that had been so kind and supportive. I hit the ground running after I came home, and my life filled up like an over-flowing cup with so many things. Yet, of course I still made time to see Victor and Cora.

Victor felt I should take my time and make some notes for myself when I could. As the weeks went by, it became very clear that this was the right course. Our quest and story was not about cashing in on some sort of trend of fad, nor to set Victor up as 'Shaman of the Year', or for me to join the ranks of the latest psychic trends, or to create another cultish end of the world movement. It was a part of a greater whole, a movement of emotions and energy to help clarify human choice and values. We are now again in need of such focus, within ourselves as well as without.

When I first recounted the story, there were some name changes, as well as alterations in the sequence of events, and a certain vagueness as to where we were at the time in Hawaii when those events occurred. This was to protect sacred sites and the people we encountered. Nevertheless, I told the story pretty much as it unfolded when it was published in the small local Feri pagan magazine '*Witcheye*'. Cora was very pleased and happy that the local Bay Area pagan community could now hear the story. At the time, that was good enough for me. Now, after so many years, not only have many people passed on, including Cora, or moved to other places in the world, but over the years, Pele has totally changed the Hawaiian landscape, especially on the big island. Places like the Queen's Bath are no more than a sweet treasured memory. Hawaii as a state wrestles with its identity as the people must also wrestle with its politics and growth. The elders, with the support of many, are making a stand for sacred sites such as Mauna Kea Hawaii's tallest Volcano. Meanwhile, America faces old challenges in new guises.

After publishing *Victor Anderson An American Shaman* and *Transpiration: Poetry & Storytelling as our Spiritual Portals*, I felt such a push to now tell the whole story of the Journey. I also realized that with the other two books out, people now had a context and better understanding of Victor and myself, in a way knowing us better as people and the times we were living in. Even though these events took place 33 years ago, their message is still very relevant. All the prayers, rites and quests that were happening all over the world at that time, and through the end of the 80s, were answered in many ways. Humanity had been given a gift and a chance to make a powerful move for our future. We HAVE made it this far, but now what? This world and the divine world await our choices that will re-tune the future.

By understanding this, *Journey for a Tomorrow* makes even more sense. The people of the United States and the rest of our world need to see not only the bigger picture of human impact on this earth, but the totality of our history and what those events and decisions mean for us now. Many others have been, and will be, called to the challenges of deep personal and cosmic work for ourselves and the world around us. This was and is as true for the ancient aborigine peoples, the times of Buddha and Jesus, the meaning behind the myths and legends of King Arthur, the mysteries of Mary and the dreams and visions some have experienced. Even today in our modern times there are those who seek to protect the helpless, heal the hopeless and stand up to evil without and within. If we craft our reality to mirror the beauty, logic and wonder of nature, we can see things for what they really are, as well as what can be.

The Beginnings

All over the world, we find various names and many stories that describe a spiritual and/or magical journey. Some of our most beloved tales, be they a fairytale, legend, epic poetry, or a historical perspective are usually rooted in some sort of journey. These personal renderings of cosmic journeys are usually based on quests unexpectedly thrust upon the person so chosen. More often nowadays, the journey appears to be one we choose ourselves. By doing so, we may shake loose from the constraints of modern life to discover the core of who we are and what it is we really want and need. We desire to understand the core of our personal internal dissatisfactions and the meaning of our existence to find full joy and satisfaction in our purpose here on earth. So, quite naturally, one type of this kind of journey is of course the internal one. Its seeking is encouraged and brought on by various means, such as deep meditation, prayer, chanting, fasting, physical stress, deep dream states, profound emotion and the use of various herbs, plants, and other substances that may help us down the paths of our quest. The journey Linda and I undertook had some internal aspects to it for me, but for both of us it was a real time physical journey. The experience of this journey was slightly different for Linda at times because she was not a student of Victor's and had been planning a vacation to Hawaii anyway. Still, Spirit knew that she was my ideal partner for this quest, because Linda loves adventure of all kinds and has a good head on her shoulders and helped me when I needed it.

The outer, real time quest journey of this kind that Linda and I were about to embark on is known by many terms in different cultures and religions. To Christians and Muslims, it's the pilgrimage. For Native Americans, it's the vision quest. The Aborigines have the walkabout. Buddhists have the *yana*, and for others it is the sacred quest or odyssey, as in the search for the Grail or the Golden Fleece. Of course, in modern times we also have the journey to find oneself. There are those who present themselves at the feet of certain teachers and disciplines. This kind of odyssey might involve a test, an initiation with perhaps an ultimate reward of some kind. Yet, it seems that at most times it is something different altogether, having been precipitated by need and a crying out from the deepest wells of consciousness itself. Spiritual quests may involve searching for the root of one's inner drives, passions and motivations to clarify one's direction or career in life. On the other hand, it can flow from a mysterious request or spiritual assignment that may come from a spiritual teacher, a god or goddess, or the great Spirit of the universe itself.

In my case, it was because both Victor and I had heard and felt the call, and both of us felt a kind of cosmic pressure on the collective destiny of humankind. He was already aware of things being amiss within the currents of our reality when I told him of my dreams and omens. He carefully looked over my notes with his big magnifying glass and asked me questions. Victor then explained that America and even the whole world was at a very critical fulcrum point in its history and that we were approaching a tipping point very quickly.

'What do you mean?' I asked. 'What kind of tipping point?'

'The kind of tipping point where humanity either rises to the need of the times because they have a rare collective understanding of the momentousness of the opportunity, or they ignore or miss it, and it all goes to hell in a handbasket.' Victor's tone was so even and objective it was as if he was standing at this fulcrum point himself. I told him so. He smiled and, closing his eyes, rocked in his rocking chair for a moment taking a deep breath, and replied, 'Cornelia, we all are. Every single human, every single living thing, even every piece of consciousness that exists in such endless ways that we see and can't see, is on the fulcrum point with us. The difference and the point...' he let out a little chuckle, '...is how aware of it you are, in this moment or any other moment, of yourself or of those around you, of the country, or even of the world.'

'So...am I being chosen? I am still in many ways a naïve girl of a woman. I don't have much money. Why don't they send you? You know so much more than me.' My statement seemed quite sensible to me.

Victor looked as sage and serene as Yoda in his rocker. 'It may not be about you the person, Cornelia, it may have to do perhaps with a certain quality you have that you might not even be fully aware of, or perhaps it could be who and/or what you are connected to that will help fulfill this purpose.'

'That still does not explain why you can't do whatever this is.' I was almost pouting, which made Victor very amused.

'What is it that I tell you to do when you need to discern the will of the gods?' he asked.

'You say to take four slow deep breaths and say the flower prayer, and then ask your High Self to open the way for you so that you may see the bigger picture of things.'

'That is correct.' Victor nodded. 'And what is the next thing?'

'The next thing is to apply logic and common sense, to ask thoughtful questions, to sound divination practices, as well as dreams and omens.'

'Very good. Let us take a moment to center ourselves.'

We took four deep slow breaths and said our prayer and after a few moments of quiet, Victor asked me 'So, what are the most interesting things about you that the gods might find useful that I may not have access to? Don't overthink it,' he added.

'Well... I can see, and that might be helpful even though you have etheric sight,'

'Indeed.' He nodded. 'Go on.'

'I have access to lots of different kinds of people. I am in pretty good shape, so I can get to places. I have a good education and am pretty well rounded that way. I have a nice smile and all in all am more patient then you are with people most times and...' I brightened. 'I'm married to a lawyer!'

Victor roared with good-natured laughter. 'Well, that about sums it up good!'

'Doesn't seem like all that much compared to other people,' I said, somewhat dryly.

'Now, now we have spoken on such feelings before, remember?' he intoned.

I sighed. 'Yes, I remember. Do not debase yourself or practice false modesty for both is a perversion of one's character and may grow to a blight on the soul.'

'Very well and poetically put.' Pleased, Victor grinned broadly. 'Now apply these things and we will see what happens'

From the time I first started seeing Victor, it did not take long for me to see that Victor's love of the Polynesian people and culture ran deep. How he respected them for the love they had for nature and their gods. That their songs, chants and rites expressed such humbleness and joy for the mysteries of life. It was and is contained in their dances, language and art, the elements that most of Western culture has lost. The unbridled joy of being alive, the passion of creative possibility, the power of innocence in love and ecstasy, as well as the culture's love and respect for nature. He felt that we, as modern people with so much information at our fingertips, and the means to easily travel the world, would learn from the rise and fall of other cultures, including that of Hawaii.

He would moan: 'The people of this earth nowadays are

in a world of gifts and blessings yet perversely we curse ourselves.'

He could also surprise me at times with how intense his sorrow and rage could be over the suffering of the animal world to satisfy human lusts and foolish needs, such as the harvesting of shark fins with the living sharks tossed back into the seas to bleed to death. He spoke of the rhino's horns being chopped or ripped off its body with no thought for the suffering this causes on so many levels.

'What do you mean, on so many levels?' I asked him. 'Surely the suffering of the dying animals that are losing fins, eyes, horns or private parts is sad enough. What other levels are there?'

I still did not fully realize how these conversations were to be a big part of my journey to come, or that this was a large part of my training in what Victor called Feri.

'Everything has a bigger picture, Cornelia. Sure, the shark, the tiger and the rhino suffer, but what of the young that also die without their parent, or those that are never born, so the future of a species dies? What about how every creature affects the land and how their loss sets chain-reactions in motion that we are only beginning to understand? How about the effect on the mind, spirit and souls of those who do such horrible things out of desperation to feed their families? The shame and sorrow they feel as their land turns to ruin around them, and they know they played a part in it. How about the governments that close their eyes to allow such cruelty as a means for these barbarities to control weapons, drugs or human trafficking, which still happens anyway? It all fits together, a puzzle of heinous human excuses and behavior that is an insult to all beauty and life on this world.'

'What can be done Victor?'

'We live, we pray, we appeal to the gods to open our eyes. We survive.'

A New Life Leading to Signs and Omens

I first spoke with Victor Anderson in late 1981. This was a turning point in my life. 1978 to 1982 had been about shedding the downy feathers of my youth and small-town life. I learned not only about city life but watched history unfold just outside my door and down the street. On the one hand, it was a time of great creativity in all the arts and the testing of boundaries on so many levels. It was colorful, exciting, in many ways an idealistic and romantic era, yet also sometimes very scary and other times sad. A time that was full of other tales and adventures and loss for me.

San Francisco was at the forefront of so many movements and trends, it was also the hotbed of political maneuvering, tragedies and intrigue from the Jim Jones and the People's Temple church and group. his group of people, led by what many considered a handsome and charismatic leader, left San Francisco with many of his followers for the country of Guyana. Soon, reports came in of bizarre behavior and abuse. The whole affair ended in a shocking mass killing, in which over 900 people committed suicide, and Congressmen Ryan, along with four other people, was shot and killed.

Not long after this came the murder of Harvey Milk and Mayor Moscone in San Francisco, with the beginnings of the Aids crisis on its heels. International drug and arms deals were also being made, with many hands being shaken under and over international tables. America seemed to be losing its moral center. Yet, at the same time open-minded ideas and spiritual elements through the entertainment field, through colleges and spiritual organizations, raised a cry for peace and understanding.

This cry and movement was debated and discussed in the gathering places and cafes of the world, through books then out on the world stage, in various ways, giving pause and reflection for change to happen. This all occurred in the midst of plane hijackings, embassy attacks, famines, wars and earthquakes. Despite this, people became more spiritually and emotionally daring, with a new kind of personal accountability to the world at large. This led to many environmental movements, new legal considerations and laws, and to new inventions. Through new technology people sought both old and new knowledge and dared to question the status quo in ways that went much deeper than the simple 'make love not war' of the 1960's and early 70's. By the 1980's, the hippies of San Francisco were embracing the tech-wave of the future or were literally heading for the hills.

By late 1981, I had been exploring the Native American movement and the rising Pagan movements of various traditions and became a metaphysical minister at The Church of Amron in San Francisco. There, I solidified my religious and philosophical education that had started in childhood and which continued through my explorative studies in college. Amron was not only ecumenical but multicultural on numerous levels. Not only did we address the wide cultural community of San Francisco, with people from all over the world, we specialized in counseling bi-racial couples and families with more than one religious background. We provided sandwiches for at risk kids in shelters and were at the forefront of the Aids crisis with resources and spiritual help, as well as visiting terminal patients at hospitals.

Like Victor, I too came from a multicultural heritage, (as I also related in my first 2017 book *Victor Anderson, an American Shaman* and in my 2018 book *Transpiration: Poetry and Storytelling as our Spiritual Portals.*) In some ways, I felt a bit more fortunate in my childhood because my family did not hide from me – as Victor's family attempted to hide from him completely – our cultural, spiritual, and traditional roots, that was mixed and grounded in a strong Christian devotion. Within my family, especially to me, stories and mystical tales were told with gusto and flourish, or were whispered as revered, sacred tales. Victor's family, especially his mother, on the other hand, wanted only to quietly melt into the American pot, and blissfully sink into the arms of the Christian church. Needless to say, the birth of Victor put a large bump in what should have been a predictable and well-paved road. The great storm that heralded Victor's birth as well as his death was also a harbinger of his fate: A passionately powerful, colorful, and star-crossed life.

My passion in the early 80s was studying folk and fairy tales, as well as learning all I could about elemental and interdimensional spirit beings, such as what we call angels. This turned into a lecture and class series I taught, which I called *Angels, Fairies and Dwarves.* Around that time, a mysterious artist (who was Anodea Judith) asked me, after one of my classes, if I'd ever heard of the fairy shaman, Victor Anderson. I said that I didn't think so. She wrote his number on a small piece of paper, told me to call him and walked away, leaving me somewhat bemused.

I called Victor that night, not sure what to expect. Within the first few words out of his mouth, I knew he could charm the fairies right out of the woods with his beautiful, resonant voice. I also then knew that my life was going to be profoundly touched by this man.

Although it is true that one of the most important missions in Victor's life was to explore and then convey to humankind our ancient spiritual history and the true nature and composition of the soul, where we started out was – I guess you could call it – 'the nature of nature.'

'The Feri path is not about gossamer wings,' Victor would thunder. 'It is a path of power, wisdom, wonder and delight. It is humankind's oldest religion but remember if you betray the essence of its principles, therein lies madness. Nature seldom gives second chances, so beware of where you tread!'

It was a time when so much changed in my life, and even though when I'd married and had seemed to settle into a typical life for a young American woman, the universe and its 'forces that be' kept nudging me to pay attention. I began having very interesting dreams and I noticed that everywhere I went, odd repetitive numbers would pop up, such as me waking up at 3:33 a.m. or my bill from the store being 11:11. In fact, 11:11 was popping up everywhere – each time I looked at the clock or the microwave, or at the laundromat wall. I then dreamed a set of numbers that seemed to signify longitude and latitude. When I looked them up, one set came up as Hawaii, and the other was on the edge of Libya, very near the borders of Tunisia and Algeria, by an ancient city called Ghadames, which had been an important trading and communication point for caravans crossing the Sahara. I also noted that these two points were close to being opposite sides of the world.

I spoke to Victor about what I was experiencing, and he told me to be patient until the meaning and message were clear. It was not long before Victor let me know how far his hand could stretch, and how the Feri way was without a doubt the religion of nature and the heart of a universal way for our world.

So many doors of various kinds opened in this time. You might have heard of the Harmonic Convergence, which was the name given to one of the world's first globally synchronized, public meditation and prayer events. This occurred on August 16–17, 1987, after the events reported in this book. The Harmonic Convergence also closely coincided with an exceptional alignment of planets.

The principal organizer of the Convergence was a man called Jose Arguelles, an American author, artist and New Age philosopher. He was also one of the originators of the Earth Day concept. Arguelles believed that the timing of the Harmonic Convergence was significant, not just to the Aztec prophecies but also to the Mayan calendar and to European, and even Asian, astrological traditions. He felt it was all connected as a part of humankind's shamanistic roots all over the world. The Convergence's dates had planetary alignments with the Sun, Moon and six out of eight planets, which were part of an important grand trine, signifying the end of one great cycle and the beginning of another. These cycles had long been spoken of historically and were presently the subject of a widespread discussion, emanating from the Americas to various cultures all over the world. Arguelles and others had felt that in that time humanity could influence its future through thought, meditation, and prayer, thus opening its hearts and collective mind to wanting a better world and increasing personal accountability for our actions in thought and deed.

I spoke with Victor about what was happening at the time, more than a year before this Convergence, letting him know about the signs, omens and dreams I'd experienced, as well as my restless confused feelings about what all this might mean.

Victor replied, 'I know', and with a smile, continued, 'I have seen that way open for you very soon and you will go to Hawaii, and you will greet the gods for me.' Victor thereafter told me that 'We will do a great working'.

At that point, I was not at all sure what that would mean, nor could I imagine how such a thing would happen.

Nevertheless, on the same evening, my phone rang. It was Linda, a friend of mine from Michigan, who I had not seen in several years. 'Hey, do you want to go to Hawaii?' she asked.

'Sure,' I blurted out in shock. 'How did you know I've been wanting to go?'

'Your name just kept coming to mind,' she answered, 'and I don't want to go alone. Besides...' Linda laughed. 'You're always good for an adventure and are resourceful even if you don't have much money.'

'I am interesting, that's for sure,' I agreed and we both laughed.

And so, the way was opened. It quickly became clear that we would also be in Hawaii for the last appearance of Halley's Comet on this cycle, which Norma, the head of Amron at the Metaphysical Church I was working for, found quite significant. The whole Church was very supportive, as were all my friends, Christian and Pagan alike. This gave me the impetus to set up a world prayer circle to coincide with the appearance of Halley's Comet in the night sky, on the 11th, at 11 at night. I contacted many people all over the world, including family, friends, those in spiritual organizations and the music business connections I had at that time, asking them to pray for peace and for human consciousness to open to more constructive possibilities, rather than destructive ones. Victor and I conversed regarding details over the next few weeks. He had a vision of where I should go when in Hawaii, and he told me that I must be on my toes because I would meet Hawaiian shamans known as *kahunas*.

Right before I left, Victor very carefully wrote something down on a small slip of paper and handed it to me. It was in Hawaiian. 'This is my Hawaiian name,' Victor explained. 'The private spiritual name of one of my past lives there. When you meet the *kahunas*, let them see this, and if they are *kahuna* or at least well-trained, they will know. Bring the paper back to me and don't let anyone else see it.'

'You keep saying *kahunas*, Victor,' I replied, my eyebrows raised slightly, 'but from what I hear, it's very hard to find *one kahuna*, let alone several.'

'They will most likely find you,' he chuckled.

Part I

An Encounter with Pele

If you have flown to Hawaii, you know what it is like to fly over the endless miles of the Pacific Ocean, with water as far as your eyes can see, then suddenly to come upon a rainbow covered emerald jewel in the middle of this great white-capped sea. It took my breath away.

After our plane had landed, Linda and I stepped into what can only be described as a slap in the face of golden sun and the powerful smell of tropical flowers. Beautiful Hawaiian girls called out '*Aloha!*' and placed a *lei* of flowers over our heads. Then we were led to an island hopper that took us to the Big Island. Once there, we quickly found out where the car rentals were.

Soon we were out of the airport and were walking towards our car. 'Where to?' asked Linda, happily sniffing her *lei* of Hawaiian flowers,

'Well... Victor said we should greet Pele first, because

she is Hawaii's mother – meaning, of the land itself. He said that there is an old story that Pele knew she needed more land far away from the people in Polynesia. This would be a new land, so with her footsteps and heart's blood she created the Hawaiian Islands that she rules over with the fire of her volcano.'

'Hmm,' mused Linda, 'so how do you greet this goddess, exactly?'

'Victor said that a special, proper *lei* must be thrown in her volcano. Also, she is very fond of gin,' I replied with a wink and twinkle, taking out from my purse and holding up an airplane miniature bottle of gin.

Linda turned on her heel.

'Where are you going?' I called after her.

'I'm going to find a liquor store and get the biggest friggin' bottle of gin I can buy. I'm not takin' any chances with a goddess who can melt rock and throw fire around.'

She left me momentarily feeling bemused and amused.

Presently, Linda returned, obviously satisfied with the quantity and quality of her purchase. Having now obtained our car we drove towards the Kilauea Volcano, which Victor had said was Pele's in-residence home, in search of a proper *lei*. We passed a sign announcing, "Visitor Center". I found myself pulling in, not sure why.

'What are you doing?' Linda exclaimed. 'This is a state sanctioned tourist trap.'

'I don't know, but I have a feeling we should pull in here,' I responded. 'At the very least, they'll have good maps.'

Like all good visitors' centers, this one was filled with exhibits. However, I barely glanced at them, drawn as I was to the information desk. Sitting there was a young woman surrounded by beautiful, sweet-smelling flower *lei*s.

I felt compelled to get straight to the point. 'Hi. I'm looking for a special *lei*.'

The young woman beamed, 'Oh, for a special occasion, for your hair, or to wear?' she asked.

'No, not for myself. You see, this is my first time in Hawaii, and I wish to properly greet Pele. To do so, I've been taught I need a proper *lei*.' I dearly hoped what I was saying made sense to her.

The young woman's mouth dropped open slightly, but she recovered quickly. 'Yes, yes, this is correct. But may I ask who taught you this?'

'Victor Anderson. He's well known in the San Francisco area as a shaman and a *kahuna*.' I added. 'He has never been to the Islands in this life, but this is where his heart is, for he says his last life was here.'

The young woman regarded me seriously. 'I must talk to my auntie about this tonight. She is a *kahuna*.'

'Well, can you memorize this name?' I responded, pulling out the small piece of paper Victor had given me. 'Do you speak Hawaiian?' I continued, hoping not to insult her.

Again, the young woman beamed a broad smile, 'Oh, yes. My auntie made sure of that.'

I showed her the name on the small piece of paper.

Her eyes widened slightly. 'Oh, my,' she said, softly. 'Come here at 11 tomorrow morning and I'll tell you what my auntie says.'

Linda and I thanked her and headed for the car. I was thrilled that we had found our first *kahuna* connection so easily and in such a random way at that.

'I have a suggestion,' said Linda as we got back in the car. 'Since we have to wait until tomorrow to properly greet Pele, why don't we make a beeline for the beach and be a proper tourist for a hot minute.'

I eagerly agreed. The weather was perfect, and we had spent long hours in a plane and a car. Some food, a warm beach and a swim sounded heavenly.

Within thirty minutes we found a beach that was not too

crowded, with gentle waves and various boats scattered about offshore. We grabbed some sandwiches and passed a tree with fruit hanging heavy and ripe over the walkway.

'Wow, mangos!' I cried. 'I've never seen them attached to a tree!' I laughed. We picked two and headed toward the water.

We found a great spot, rubbed each other with sun-tan lotion and started to arrange our food on the blanket. I found myself looking up suddenly: that instant reaction almost impossible to control when you feel someone is staring at you. I was looking back into silver-mirror aviator sunglasses and wearing them was a very handsome man somewhere between thirty and thirty-eight years old.

'Checking out the hunks already?' The amusement crackled through Linda's voice.

I felt the color rush to my cheeks. 'No,' I denied softly. '*He* was staring at *us*.'

'Oh, really!' A mischievous catlike grin flashed across Linda's face, turning into an inviting smile, followed by a big wave. 'Hey! you hungry?' she called out to the man.

The man flashed back an engaging smile. He got up

from his spot on the sand and walked over. He did not have the air of a tourist about him but nor that of a local white guy either. Still, the tan was deep, the hair a sun-kissed light brown, the eyes – when he took his aviators off – a gentle blue. Linda offered him half a sandwich and a big slice of mango. He seemed sincerely grateful as we exchanged pleasantries. He wolfed down his food, so while Linda and I still munched on ours, he told us about himself as much as he felt like sharing. He spoke of the rat race of the mainland and that when he had come to Hawaii on vacation five years before he'd made the decision to drop kick his life and move to Hawaii for good. He sold everything he had and bought a boat.

'And there she is,' he said, pointing toward the ocean and a good-sized sailboat. 'Now, I take people out on the water to fish or to watch whales or just sight-see. Most of the time it's great fun.'

'But sometimes it must suck,' added Linda.

'I'm not a fan of drunk idiots on any boat, let alone mine.' The handsome man's tone had gone quite dry.

I gave him a warm smile. 'Yet, what makes it worth it with the idiots is that you can see the beauty around you, even if they can't.'

He fell silent for a minute, staring deeply into me for a minute and seemed to come to some sort of decision. 'So, what's your story, girls? Just on college vacation?'

I laughed 'No, not quite. Linda works in the law field and I'm married, but at the moment we're here on a spiritual quest. We've not even asked your name or offered ours. This is Linda, I'm Cornelia.'

He brightened again and extended his hand 'And I'm Frank. How do you do.'

We all laughed.

Frank stood up. 'I'd like to thank you for the food by giving you a sail for an hour or two. I can drop you off closer to shore.'

My eyebrows shot up. Linda and I looked at each other as Frank quickly added, 'You don't have to worry about anything. I'm not looking for beach bunnies; those are a dime a dozen around here. I have everything you need on ship.'

Linda shielded her eyes looking out at the sailboat. 'How we getting out there? I'm a real good swimmer. How about you Cornelia?'

'Oh, I'm a valiant dog-paddler. I could do it,' I said, good naturedly blushing a little.

'I wear my flippers real tight, so they'll fit you,' offered Frank after glancing at my feet.'

Linda and I ran back to the car with our stuff. 'I assume you're getting good vibes off this guy?' she asked.

'Hey, you're the one who waved him over, but yeah... There's more to his story, though, but it's not our business.'

'What do you think it is?'

I shrugged. 'It's something in the way he moves. Looks maybe like an ex-cop or soldier. He's working through something. He's a fair guy, and we made him curious and we were kind.'

We quickly locked up and found him waiting on the beach, flippers in hand. He indicated I sit down, and he fitted a flipper on my foot.

'No glass slippers for this Cinderella,' I chuckled.

'Nope, but we will turn you into a mermaid. Once they're wet, they'll fit firmly. Just kick normally and you will be amazed how quickly they'll move you through the water.' He pulled the flipper off and once in the water helped me get them on.

He was right. Swimming with the flippers was a joyous feeling. It took all of one minute for me to get used to them.

We swam at a slow steady pace. The water was perfect. 'I'm surprised that the water is so calm,' I said. 'I was expecting big waves.'

'That all depends on which island you're on, or which beach or what time of year,' Frank answered as he did a gentle sidestroke.

Even though the sailboat had looked quite far away, we arrived quickly. Frank climbed easily up a ladder at the end of what was a 38 to 40-foot sailboat. He gave Linda and I a hand up. Looking back to shore was breathtaking for now we had a panoramic view of the island.

'Wow!' I called out to him. He nodded smiling and started releasing the sails.

Do they have sail boats in heaven? I thought to myself. I could not imagine a more happy or peaceful feeling. I took it all in while Frank let Linda take the wheel. The sails filled with a gentle, warm puff of wind and we were off.

Frank shouted instructions and pointed to various spots on shore. He seemed happy to share the moment with some people who were genuinely interested in what he had to say.

The wind died down and Frank indicated this was a

good spot to swim and snorkel. He had all necessary equipment including some fins for Linda.

'Any sharks?' asked Linda

'Not usually around here but they can show up anywhere. You know, it's their ocean. Still, I wouldn't worry, lots of natural food here. They very seldom bother people. As long as you're not bleeding,' he added looking over his glasses.

The eyes of each of us must have been as wide as children's, as we looked at each other and both answered him 'Nope! No bleeding here!'

Which made him laugh. 'I'll stay topside and keep watch. If you've never snorkeled before, don't dive too deep. It's a long way down here,' he cautioned. 'At least seventy to a hundred feet.'

Once we were in the water, Linda gave me a few pointers concerning the snorkel, such as the old spitting in the face mask and rinsing trick which supposedly helps keep the face plate clear. The first thing we did was swim under the boat, which instantly reminded me of the old TV show *Sea Hunt*. Once I felt secure with myself around the sailboat, I turned my attention and vision out and under water. The water was astonishingly clear, but I could tell the bottom was far away because I had been warned, otherwise one could fall for the illusion that it was easily reachable. As I looked out into the distance, I could see a school of fish swimming maybe about a football field's length away. Then I mentally gasped for very far away in the shadowy distance was something very large. Maybe a whale but too far away to really tell. I turned to look in other directions and was greeted by miles of endless sea. Linda and I swam to the surface and pulled up our snorkel masks to talk.

'This is so different from the lakes in Michigan or the east coast. It's like another country,' she said.

I agreed that it was just what it felt like.

We swam back up to the boat where Frank was watching. 'If you're ready to come up, I have some snacks and something to drink before we head back,' he offered.

On board again, we wrapped ourselves in beach towels and nibbled various chips. Frank nestled a beer in his hands, while Linda and I settled for cold cans of soft drinks.

I decided to take a shot and asked, 'This is quite the life you've built for yourself here. Will it be enough in the long run?'

The sunglasses were back on, so I could not see his eyes. 'I really don't know,' Frank answered. 'Hawaii has been very good to me. I couldn't imagine leaving but I try not to think of the future.'

I took a deep breath and replied, 'I'm very lucky to have found a man who not only trusts me but allows me to be myself, and grow the way I want to, and believes me when I say I have a cosmic assignment in Hawaii, no less.'

Frank chuckled 'Yes, you *are* lucky, for such a man is either a soulmate, like these New Age people call it, or he's a fool.'

'Well, he's a lawyer, so he's no fool, but we took the time to really get to know each other. What ties us together is not things or children but what we value and care about philosophically.'

'Ah, so is that the secret?' Frank took off his glasses and looked at me.

I found myself blushing again a bit. 'It helps to be a reasonably cute cupcake and know how to cook,' I offered.

Frank burst out laughing and got to his feet, clearing the little table. 'I'll take this under advisement.' He winked.

The wind picked up again and I got the feeling that Frank already knew it would, being fully aware of the rhythms and timing of this place. He was whistling as he took the wheel. I was blessed by a quick flash of dolphins in the water on the way back. He took us as close as he could to shore so it would be an easy swim back. We exchanged warm goodbyes and thanked Frank for a lovely time. We waved from the beach and as we walked away Linda mused, 'That was an amazing experience. He was quite the hunk, but this was not about that. Do you think it was all about him needing to hear about what you said to him?'

I was thoughtful a moment before answering. 'I think it was partly that, but something also tells me that somehow it was also a test of some kind. Maybe for all of us.'

Grateful for a good night's sleep, the scent of flowers in the Hawaiian air was also almost like a drug, so we slept deeply till the next morning. Though a little jet lagged we still managed to be at the Visitor Center promptly at 11 a.m. The young woman jumped up as we walked up to her stand.

'Here, this is for you,' she said, with warmth and pride in her voice.

It was our turn to be open-mouthed as the young woman handed us a large, hefty, green and intricately woven leaf *lei*. 'My auntie was working on this as I walked in. She told me that she foresaw your coming and made this ready for you. This is her gift to you and Pele. This is a traditional *lei* for an offering to Pele, especially to her. She told me that your journey and your work is blessed. Now, I will show you where you must go.'

On a map the young woman carefully drew directions to Kilauea's crater. 'There is a wooden guard rail here,' she explained, pointing. 'This is where the locals go over the rail to throw in their offerings. The wind can throw things back at you sometimes so watch for that. But be careful. Pele does not care for human offerings – unless you are virgins, of course,' she concluded, teasingly with a playful wink.

We all laughed. Thanking her and her auntie profusely, Linda and I left the Visitor Center, now fully armed and ready to meet the Goddess Pele.

Heading towards Kilauea, we soon saw signs for the Volcano House. This time we were both curious, and Linda and I made a quick stop at this splendid Victorian mansion, now part restaurant and part museum.

It was here that we first saw Pele in her many forms. Depicted in a painting over a hundred years old, a very romantic Pele rose from the flames, naked in her womanly and fiery glory. Yet it was a large blow-up of a famous photograph that gave us considerable pause. The photograph was truly awe-inspiring; the volcano was captured exploding in billowing fury. In the middle of all this power, and made of the smoke itself, was the serene face of a beautiful woman. We stared at this picture for a while when a formal looking waiter came up to us. He greeted us when we asked him about the photo and shared with us a few tales of Pele, illustrating her volcanic ways and the Hawaiian people's love and devotion to her even in these modern times, this all before asking if we were staying for lunch.

Pele by Arthur Johnsen

We told him no, that we were on our way to the crater.

'Oh, good,' the waiter responded in approval, then cautioned us to be aware that while Pele loves the good-hearted and innocent, she is deeply offended by those who take her lava rocks from the site of her sacred volcano. She punishes those who do, and the Ranger Station as well as the Volcano House, hold mute testament to this in the form of thousands of lava rocks that have been returned by mail from all over the world. A large pile of those rocks lay to the side of the front door with a sign explaining why they were there.

'We now take any rock mailed to us and drive it up to her every few months.' The waiter grinned. He also warned us not to take any of Pele's hair that we might find on the ground and instructed us to always give an old woman a ride if we see one, because this is Pele's favorite disguise, one that tests people's spirits and woe to those who fail!

Taking all this to heart, Linda and I thanked the kind waiter and started on our way. We drove towards the crater. As we moved upwards, we were captured by the contrast of beauty and desolation, side by side. We saw seemingly impenetrable rock that had been cracked open by short trees with lava-red flowers. Grey and black stones and dead wood meeting an azure blue sky.

Mesmerized, we stopped the car and walked out to the hardened flow of what had once been molten lava.

'There are no hot spots out here?' Linda asked.

'No, not here,' I replied. 'Remember, the waiter saying that even though Pele steams it's been quite a while since the Goddess's last eruption, and even the tremors have been few and far between.' We walked a little further out, mindful of the direction of our rental car.

However, a glimmer caught my eye in the distance. This glimmer quickly turned into sparkle, and soon all over the ground at our feet were long, fine golden threads blowing about like either small golden tumbleweeds or long floating gossamer in the light breeze. This was Pele's hair, volcanic fibers that are just one of many wonders to come out of the volcano.

Linda and I tiptoed back to the car and resumed our journey. As we neared the summit, we were hit by the loathsome, frightening smell of pure sulfur. *Little wonder it is associated with hell.* To our surprise, and somewhat to our dismay, we watched the wind blow away fog-like puffs of smoking sulfur to reveal several large tourist buses at a parking lot. Several dozen people were milling about.

'How are we going to do this?' queried Linda. 'The locals must do their thing at night, or close it off, or something.'

We decided to park and discreetly take our bag of offerings towards the crater and see what would happen. The stench was overpowering but cleared to some extent as we approached the guardrail and joined people taking pictures there. It was amazing, and somewhat intimidating, to see such a gigantic gray smoking hole in the earth!

The wind suddenly shifted, and we were covered in the suffocating sulfur smoke. The tourists, gagging, ran for their buses, and once they were on board, all of them zoomed away at the same time.

Linda was grinning from ear to ear. 'I guess Pele wants her gin.'

We waited until the buses were completely out of sight before we climbed carefully through the guardrail to stand by a very scraggly looking little tree hanging on with great determination to the edge of Kilauea's mouth. Even more carefully, Linda and I looked over the side. A deep silence greeted us as we looked far down in the crater where we could see the remains of many kinds of *leis* and the shattered broken glass of even more gin bottles.

Linda shouted into the crater 'I am not throwing this bottle down there, Pele. I will not pollute your sacred mouth.'

'Volcanoes do make glass, you know,' I offered.

'I don't care. She's going to have to take it straight up.' And with no further ado, Linda opened the big gin bottle. With one hand I grabbed the sturdy little tree and with the other we locked wrists as Linda hung slightly over the edge and poured the gin out of the bottle in great hiccupping glugs.

It was now my turn. I cleared my throat and took a deep breath while stepping up to the edge. Linda remained where she was, standing close.

'I bring you greetings from Victor, your priest!' I called out.

There was silence and a breath of fresh wind from somewhere. I carefully started to speak:

'Oh, mighty Pele, hear me for I bring to you greetings from thy Priest and *Kahuna,* who in this life is called Victor Anderson. We honor you and adore the land that is your home. We come in respect, we come in love. We come to ask your favor and blessing on the work we wish to do here.'

I then spoke some words in Hawaiian that Victor wanted me to say and heaved the wreath, with all my strength, into the volcano. The faintest thud echoed up the sides. There was a great sighing sound, and then a slowly increasing rumbling as the ground beneath our feet started to tremble and shake.

I leapt away from the lip of the crater and vaulted over the guardrail in the blink of an eye.

Linda was right behind me. 'Damn!' she said, 'I never knew you had it in you to move so fast.'

'Inspiration is a wonderful thing – let alone abject terror,' I replied.

Pele sent up a big belch of smoke behind us.

We both laughed, but our eyes were still as big as saucers as we started our return to the car.

'I guess Pele liked the offering and has given us – as well as Victor – her answer. When we get back to the hotel, we must call him,' I suggested.

Linda climbed into the car, chuckling to herself. 'Wanted a vacation and got to meet a goddess. That's pretty good for just one day,' she said with satisfaction, moving back the passenger seat and pulling her hat down over her eyes. 'Yep, for one day that's real damn good. Victor should be happy with this one.' She grabbed the brim of her Indiana Jones-type hat and peeked out at me from under its rim. 'Told you we needed a big bottle, and opening it for her was just, well, polite. You talk to them; I bring the party supplies.'

'Sounds like a real good deal.' I laughed as we sped down the mountain back toward the slowly setting sun-kissed sea.

We spent the about 2 days with some friends where we were able to enjoy the music and night life of Hawaii. It was delightful to see how much the people of the islands loved all music and could easily dance to modern rock music to jazz to modern Hawaiian. All the dancing and deep sleep during the day got rid of any jet lag we had, so we were bright eyed and ready to hop over to Maui. It was calling to me somehow and I wondered what adventures awaited.

Part II

The Boy Who Knew

'It is good! It is very good,' Victor's voice beamed over the phone lines. 'You have Pele's blessing and protection with you now. The next thing you must do is to pray to Uli, her sister. You must first swim in her sacred waters. The next *kahuna* you will meet you'll speak with directly. Tell her what I have taught you. Speak of the *Menehune* and the doors will be opened for you.'

'But where do we go now, Victor?' I asked. 'There's water everywhere; oceans, rivers, pools with rainbows around every corner. How will we know which one?'

'Spirit will lead you. The gods will guide and protect you. Go as far as you can away from the busy tourist places. Find sacred waters and ask for those who know the oldest stories. Remember to tell and show the *kahunas* my Hawaiian name,' Victor instructed.

After a deep and peaceful sleep, Linda and I got up early and consulted our maps. The densest parts of Hawaii's population clustered on certain coastal sections as they did on many of the other Pacific islands. As one travels further away from the coast, the roads often turn into single twisty lanes. The maps warned us to drive slowly, and some of them advised using only four-wheel drive on certain roads.

'Looks like this is the general direction we need to head towards,' Linda pointed out on the map. 'But before we venture out into the jungle, I want to catch a few rays on the more mundane side of the island... There must be someplace where we can get naked and sun worship for a while,' she mused.

I knew better than try to talk Linda out of this, so we grabbed our suntan lotion and headed out. Once outdoors, we could see in one direction clusters of hotels and resorts, but the other consisted of a long stretch of emptier looking coast. We jumped into our car and headed in this direction. The further we drove, the wilder the beach appeared, with big black boulders thrown up like a makeshift cliff. This area was considerably and significantly more rugged than the usual Hawaiian tourist beaches. We stopped and started to climb down, going over the rocks to get closer to the sand and water. Suddenly, the wind lashed my hair like a whip across my body. We dove behind the largest rock we could find.

'This must be why there are no hotels or tourists here. The wind must be like this most of the time,' I gasped, snuggling into a shielded corner with Linda.

'You're most likely right, but I'm not letting a little wind stop me,' Linda said with renewed determination. 'Somewhere out there is a little sheltered place where we can lie down. The earth behind us, the sun on top of us... What could be more sacred than that?' she twinkled.

'You know, we never even bothered to ask at the hotel if nude sunbathing is allowed or even legal here,' I said, half to myself.

The air in our safe little pocket exploded with Linda's strong feelings on the matter, which ended with, '...and it sure as hell should be legal here, if anywhere in the US of A.'

'True, true...' I nodded but could not help adding, 'but there *is* that little matter of those well-meaning pesky Victorian Christians who have left their mark here, you know.'

Undaunted, Linda grunted and, with me following, threw herself back into the biting wind. After some maneuvering, we found a small patch of warm, peaceful sand surrounded by a small cove of cliff rocks. We appeared to be very much alone except for what looked like a fishing line that stretched from the top of the outcropping of rocks above us far out into the rolling waves. We looked at each other with the same thought: Had this line just been left here for some reason or was there someone on the other end? Without a word, we started to climb up to investigate. Peering carefully over the rocks, we spied a quite beautiful boy, almost a young man, who at first glance appeared be fifteen, even maybe sixteen or so. He was quite the picture of youthful perfection. Linda let out a soft low purr and started to move toward him. I grabbed her belt and pulled her back down beside me.

'Whoa there, woman! Let's not stalk the locals, especially if they look like jailbait!' I laughed.

Linda narrowed her amber cat eyes at me. 'You know... It's just a matter of style, and of course desire. You tend to like them younger or older and they buzz around you like bees. I personally don't care about the *age* at all,' she drawled, 'as long as they're legal, to my taste and I get to hunt them down.' She grinned wickedly, adding, 'With appreciation and love in my lustful heart, of course.'

'Of course,' I replied with a twinkle in my own eyes. 'I certainly wouldn't want to deny anyone the opportunity of your or even my "appreciation", but don't you think it's a little odd that on this huge windy beach we're the only ones here? Maybe he has information for us.'

'OK. OK,' Linda relented, good-naturedly. 'I'll be sweet and meek. Besides, you're right – he does look a little young. *But,* are you sure the ghosts of those pesky Christians aren't affecting your basic pagan nature?' she teased.

Somehow, I allowed myself to get a little flustered. 'Really, Linda! Being pagan does *not* mean you don't have self-control or morals. You can't think that Pele gives you permission to pounce on any boy like a cat on a mouse!'

'Probably not,' she laughed, 'but it works for me. Isn't there that "do what thou wilt shall be the whole of the Law" thing, hmm?'

'That was Crowley, and he's another ball of wax,' I shot back.

'Don't worry,' Linda uttered reassuringly, then intoning. 'He's yours to do with as you will...'

'Oh, what horseshit!' I laughed and turned to climb back up. We popped our heads over the rocks and were greeted by a devastatingly bright smile.

'*Aloha*! Hope we didn't scare you popping up like this,' I said, smiling.

'*Aloha*, not at all,' the beautiful boy answered graciously. 'But it was kinda unexpected. Tourists usually don't come to this beach because of the winds.'

'Oh... so, us being tourists is really obvious,' frowned Linda.

'Well, only because I grew up here and know just about everyone. Plus, you're not yet quite up to speed to pass yourselves off as being from here.

'No, I guess not.' I grinned back after scanning my arms, dearly hoping that my nose had not yet turned red.

'So, what brings you here?' the boy asked, rather directly.

I realized, as I looked deep into his dark intelligent eyes, that this young person was no fool. He was by nature open-minded and easygoing but could not be easily fed baloney. He most likely had very little need for protection from Linda or anybody else for that matter. Before I could answer him, Linda did. 'We wanted to find a nice peaceful little spot to get naked and sunbathe.'

'Oh…!' He laughed, again flashing his brilliant smile. 'Well, you found the only nice little hidden spot on this beach where you can do that!'

'Did you think we were going to smoke or ask you for weed?' I asked for some reason, wanting to know if my gut feeling was right.

'Well, it's not like I haven't been asked that before,' he chuckled, blushing ever so slightly.

'We're not those kinds of *Haoles*,' I said, throwing in the Hawaiian word for foreigner and giving him a little wink.

'No, but you're some kind of *Hapa Haole*.' He grinned. 'I can tell. I'm a quarter kid myself.' He glanced at our pinkening skin.

'Quarter or half white person?' I asked.

'Yeah… quarter Hawaiian, quarter Portuguese, quarter English, quarter Philippine,' the boy explained.

'Oh, I see. I guess that does makes me a quarter type person too except mine is continent native, German and Spanish,' I replied, feeling more at ease. 'And in your way, I guess that makes you a half and half,' I teased Linda.

'This half and this half,' she responded, with one hand on her belly and the other on her butt, 'wants to get naked before my nose burns off.'

'Well, go right on down and go for it,' the boy invited. 'You don't have to worry about the windows in that spot and I'll keep watch for you.'

'Now that's mighty friendly and Hawaiian of you,' retorted Linda, with dry humor.

I looked at her in shock because I thought she was bordering on being rude.

She tugged at her hat and shot me a look before saying. 'Now, now don't get all Mom on me. It's just what the hell is he talking about windows out here?'

The young man pointed to the hotels, way in the distance.

'Those got to be at least a mile and a half or more away from here,' snorted Linda.

'That's true, but if you stand here long enough, you'll start to see the flashes of telescopes. The nude beach used to stretch from the hotel to almost here, but they built a retirement home near that hotel and our local little old ladies didn't approve of the show, so they put a stop to it,' the boy explained.

'So, it's not legal to nude sunbathe anymore because of that?' I asked.

'I don't think it's legal or illegal, you just have to be cool about it. Which is why I offered to be a lookout for your determined friend here.'

The boy, looking the young man very much now, turned fully toward Linda. 'You don't have to worry, I won't peek. I'm sure you don't have anything I haven't seen before, plus my grandfather taught me good manners.' This came across a little pointedly as he turned to test his line.

'Well, I'm sure you got an eye full growing up here and that your grandfather taught you well. Nice to have met you and thanks for the info,' Linda replied, slightly chagrined and turning to go. 'I'm heading down.'

'I have a few more questions, if you don't mind,' I said to him as I gave Linda the "I'll be down in a minute" look.

'Shoot away. I was obviously meant to be at your service,' he responded, a smile tugging at the corners of his mouth, as he squatted down, perhaps to hide what I thought was a full grin. He turned back and took the lid off a bucket at his feet. The bucket was stuffed with fat wriggling fish.

'Wow! You have really been catching fish here!' I blurted out, impressed by his catch.

He laughed heartily and stood up. 'What did you think? That I'm up here waiting for nude sunbathers?'

Once again, I was surprised. How could he be so young and so self-assured? I decided to get to the point. 'I'm sort of doing this project. I need to find tellers of old Hawaiian stories. I need to find *kahunas*.' I said a little hesitantly.

'A college type project?' he asked, with a raise of his eyebrows.

'I could say that but it's more like a quest,' I answered truthfully. 'It has purpose; it's not idle curiosity either,' I quickly added.

'You know, there are two things you know for certain growing up here,' he stated, reeling in a fish. 'One is that you don't mess with Pele, (amen to that, I thought to myself), and the other is be very careful and respectful of the old ones, because you don't always know who is or is not a *kahuna*. I'll tell you a little story. The government wanted to build a highway all around this island to make it easy for them to get around and build more hotels. The *kahunas* cursed the project. So many things went wrong that the government had no choice but to just up and quit. Left it all behind, and that was about five years ago. They won't try again, at least for another ten years, says my grandfather, and I'm sure he's right. So, are you real sure that you need to find a *kahuna*?' The boy raised his eyebrows.

'Yes, my teacher sent me. He's a priest, a *kahuna* himself,' I confided.

The young man looked at me thoughtfully for a moment before speaking. 'On this island, they mostly live on the other north side. Which was one of the reasons they didn't want the highway built. Did your teacher give you any other instructions?'

'He said that I needed to find sacred waters.'

The handsome boy nodded in apparent understanding. 'On the other side of the island are sacred pools. They're somewhat famous but not overrun with tourists because most don't like the long drive, and it's the off-season. I would head out there, if I were you, and ask around. You just might find what you're looking for.'

'That is so helpful.' I beamed. 'Thank you so much for all your kindness. I better get back to my friend, so "thank you and blessed be", as we would say.'

'I'll throw a rock toward the other side of the cove to let you know when I'm leaving. So, "*mahalo* and *aloha*", as we say. He smiled back warmly.

Down at the beach, Linda was all laid out, looking toasty and happy. I stripped and lay down beside her. The pounding of the waves made it feel like the earth was rocking me and I drifted off into a meditative nap. All too soon we were startled by the sharp, swift hit of stone upon stone.

'Time to go.' I yawned. 'He's leaving, and we don't want to be burnt to a crisp on our first day.'

We quickly dressed.

As Linda and I clambered back to the road and to our car, we spied in the distance our young gallant Hawaiian knight walking away, fishing pole in one hand and easily swinging his bucket of fish in the other. I realized at that moment that we hadn't even exchanged names.

Part III

On the Road to Uli

In Hawaii, one has only to drive a few miles and the terrain may completely change. We were now on an intensely winding road, and it seemed that the the vegetation became thicker and lusher with every turn. The air felt heavy with the smells of damp earth, dripping greenery and the exploding color and scents of some exotic or rare bloom. There was little traffic, and what we did see was mostly local. We determined this from the confident speed of the vehicles zooming past us. So as not to miss any local flavor, we pulled over and paused next to a beautiful statue of the Virgin Mary set on an altar of rocks at a sharp curve in the road. She was covered with fresh flower *lei*s and had fruit and candle offerings at her feet.

'Guess this is some kind of dead man's curve,' offered Linda.

'Could be,' I replied. 'But remember that to many Hawaiians the Virgin Mary is another way of portraying their Hawaiian mother goddess, Uli, even though some think of her as the goddess of dark magic. Victor said this is misunderstood – just like death. Death and darkness are no more evil than the night sky or the darkness of the womb. He told me that this is also how it is with the Mexican goddess Tonantzin. She's seen now as the Virgin Mary Lady of Guadalupe.' As we got back into the car, I added, 'At least it looks like we're heading in the right direction, though.'

We were now long past the little town which had come somewhat close to resembling anything modern. We were gliding through the colorful shaded landscape, yet occasionally a break in the jungle would expose bright rolling green fields with fat happy cattle. Our car became the panning camera, sweeping from one scene to the next through the twists and curves of the road. We finally popped into a clearing, and there, in a pull-off by the road, sat a sheriff's car. The sheriff himself was over at another car with what looked like elderly tourists. He was waving instructions for them in a friendly manner. Something about him struck me, so I pulled over and stopped.

'Why are we sitting here?' inquired Linda.

'We're going to ask that sheriff some questions,' I answered.

'Well… if that's the case, I'll take this big 'ole hunting knife here and discreetly shove it into the glove compartment,' drawled Linda.

I nodded with approval. 'I see you're finally taking my advice on not terrifying the locals,' I chuckled.

Before Linda could answer the sheriff noticed us. He waved the people in the other car on their way and came over to where we were stopped.

I greeted him first. Even though much of his face was hidden behind big aviator glasses I saw that he was a handsome Hawaiian man.

'And *aloha* to you.' He leaned on the passenger window and glanced us over in a friendly professional manner. 'And what can I do for you young ladies?' he asked.

'*Aloha!*' I answered. 'We're looking for these pools that we've heard are sacred.'

The sheriff nodded and smiled. 'Just keep right on going. They're about another half mile down the road. There's also a campsite nearby. Don't drive too fast or you'll miss it,' he cautioned.

I continued, 'Since they are, after all, sacred, we'd like to know if there's anything in local custom that we should do or not do, as the case may be.'

His eyebrows arched over the aviator glasses. 'In all my

years here, I've never heard a mainlander ask such a thing.'

'Well,' I responded, 'to our way of thinking it only makes sense that if you're wandering in another country and you're friendly and polite to the local people, it should only follow that you do the same with the local gods. Seems like the right thing to do...' I added, somewhat hesitantly.

The sheriff seemed frozen and did not move for what seemed like a long moment. He then said, slowly, 'It's very nice of you to be so considerate but we have local people that take care of the thoughtless sins of the tourists. If you really wish to greet one of our gods, Pele is very open to visitors.'

'Been there, done that,' interjected Linda matter-of-factly. 'I think Pele likes us. We're now here to speak to her sister Uli and she,' Linda continued while pointing at me, 'needs to find a *kahuna*.' Linda grinned up at the sheriff, 'Thought I'd cut to the chase 'cus I'm starving and want to find some meat.'

The sheriff bowed his head for a second. 'Now you guys wouldn't be pulling my leg or belong to some wacky cult?'

'No, of course not,' I replied, trying to sound self-assured. 'We're not any more so than the Hawaiian faith being some wacky, old-fashioned pagan religion.'

The sheriff nodded, 'True, true, you got me there.' His grin was still in place. 'Are you ladies going to be camping overnight out here?'

'Yes, that's most likely what we're going to do,' I said trying to muster up my friendliest tone, while in the back of my mind I had visions of Hawaiian cops hiding in the bushes with binoculars focused on us.

'Well, then, let's see if I can help you find a nice little spot. Have a map?' he asked.

I looked over on the dash and around me 'Oh, it's in the glove compartment.' I said cheerfully, starting to reach over, when Linda caught my eye and it hit me.

The "oh shit" look must have been plain on my face because the sheriff's grin widened and in the most casual friendly tone you can imagine said, 'Oh, please, let me help,' and flipped open the glove compartment. With a metallic clunk out plopped Linda's 10-inch hunting knife in all its glory, since she was wearing the sheath. One eyebrow arched over the aviator glasses.

'It's a hunting knife,' stated Linda. 'Brought it along 'cos it's useful and because we're girls... ahh women, protection you know...'

'I see.' The sheriff eyed the knife quietly for a few moments, considering, before continuing with, 'That's a mighty big 'ole knife there. You could kill a bear with that thing. Maybe you didn't know we don't have bears in Hawaii,' he intoned hopefully, looking briefly at me and back to Linda, 'So, who does the knife belong to?'

Linda raised her hand.

'Now, why does that not surprise me?' He leaned in the window slightly, 'Young lady, are you familiar with the laws regarding concealed weapons?'

'Now, officer, the only person I was trying to conceal this from was some stupid kid trying to rip it off. I really do use it. Those little ridges there are for gutting fish and with the other edge I pop clams. I wasn't even planning on sacrificing any chickens with it.'

I felt my head softly hit the steering wheel. 'Wrong islands, different culture, Linda,' I said dryly.

The grin seemed eternally plastered on the sheriff's face. 'Well, you would be well prepared, nonetheless,' he observed.

'Look, sheriff,' I said a little exasperated, 'she really does know how to use it properly. We're originally from Michigan and there's a lot of hunting there, fish, ducks, deer and, yes, bear, but I don't think she ever skinned a bear . . . have you?' I asked Linda, dearly hoping that if she had she would have the good sense to say no.

'Naw... helped skin a deer once, but never a bear.' Linda patted her tummy. 'Like I said before I'm getting mighty hungry. I sure wouldn't mind hunting down some wild pig, though.'

'Now I'd like to see that,' said the sheriff showing more teeth. 'I've hunted wild goat and pig here myself. Really rough terrain out there and pigs can fight back. You see, by our custom, it's the men that do the hunting.' He straightened up and stretched a little. 'Young lady, why don't you get out of the car and show me your license and open the trunk?'

'What!' exclaimed Linda. 'You don't believe what she said, and you're not going to ask her for her license? She's the driver!'

'Oh, I believe her just fine. You're the one with the oversized toothpick. Now, let's open that trunk,' the sheriff ordered kindly.

Linda, with no more ado, got out the car and opened the trunk while the sheriff studied her license.

'So, you really are from Michigan,' he teased, looking us over.

Linda squirmed between being amused and disgusted. 'Of course, we are, only she,' pointing at me, 'now lives in California.'

'Well, well. Good friends on a trip together. So, why don't we take that sheath off your belt, put that nice hunting knife in it, and the knife and sheath into whatever bag holds your camping equipment back in this trunk here,' he instructed.

'Yes, sir,' Linda relented as she bounded to her task. The sheriff came around to my side of the car, leaned into the window, taking off his sunglasses and looking deep into my eyes. His eyes were dark golden-brown pools that said this sheriff takes his work very seriously, and that he was not a man to be trifled with. Nevertheless, the eyes also expressed amusement. 'Now, what is this about a *kahuna*?'

he asked more seriously, and, for the first time, the grin relaxed a little in his face.

I explained my role in this adventure. 'I'm supposed to find those *kahunas* that tell the oldest stories. I've been sent on this quest from my teacher, Victor Anderson, who is also a *kahuna* but lives in California. He told me that a true *kahuna* would recognize his name and that would be all the introduction I'd need. We really have paid our respects to Pele; we even gave her a proper *lei*.'

'Oh really? What kind of *lei* was that?' the sheriff asked.

'One of green leaves that was made for us by this young woman's auntie, who is, we were told, a *kahuna*. She informed her niece that she knew we were coming and was already making the *lei* for us. She also knew Victor's name,' I added.

'When was this?' the sheriff inquired.

'Just yesterday,' I replied. 'Right before that little earthquake they had up there at the crater.'

The sheriff straightened up, nodding to himself. Leaning towards me again, he advised, 'I think Auntie Bee will be the one to help you. She'd also enjoy speaking with you, I think.' The grin came back to the sheriff's face, and he gave more detailed instructions as to where to camp, finally telling us, 'After you set up, keep going down this road. She's on the left side in one of the few private houses. If you see a bunch of road equipment by a wall, you've gone too far, so turn around. Come back if you can't find it; for then it's not meant to be. If you do, you'll be led in. Just go up to the door and tell her I sent you. Have a nice evening and if you need any more help, just ask any local to tell you where Henry is, and I'll be right there.'

We drove off. I looked up at the sky and could feel the mid-afternoon sun on my face. Even though we'd started our day early in the morning, it seemed that time moved slower here. *It should be later in the day*, I thought to myself, *because so much has already happened*. Little did I know that my day had only just begun.

We found the entrance to the pools, and the campsite was tucked away where we were told it would be. Linda seemed very quiet. She walked around a bit and said;

'I don't want to set up camp in the open. I feel a shift in the weather coming.'

We drove the car farther into the park, got out and surveyed the scene. I looked up at the sky and saw bright patches of glowing azure blue mixed with white billowing clouds, with darker gray clouds in the distance, far away over the ocean.

'Yeah, I think you're right,' I said.

'You need to go and find that *kahuna* woman while I set up camp,' Linda suggested.

'Still, that leaves you doing all the work. Are you sure you'll be OK?' I asked.

'I'll be happy as a clam and even more so if you can find me some meat to roast.' With that, Linda started unloading the car. When satisfied that she had all she needed, she wished me, 'Happy *kahuna* hunting.' As I drove off, she shouted, 'And don't forget the meat!'

I drove off, determined to keep track of my surroundings. I had only driven a short way when it seemed that the enveloping jungle had become thicker than ever. In the back of my mind, I recalled Sheriff Henry saying that it was about two or so miles to where I needed to go, so I kept glancing at my mileage meter, checking on how far I had come. He was also right that it did not feel or look like anyone lived out here, but I supposed there must be some places tucked away, because occasionally I spotted a little road that would quickly disappear into the jungle. The dark of the thick foliage made it feel like I was fast losing the light, so I upped my speed a little. I noted a road on the left that seemed to lead to a house but that was the only one so far, so I kept going. After a while, the road brightened ahead but it still felt like a shock when the sun hit me full in the face. Now, I was driving with a cliff on one side and a wall facing the ocean on the other. There were dug out patches of turn-offs that had large highway equipment parked in them looking very much like frozen mechanical monsters. The hairs on the back of my neck started to tingle. This was what the handsome boy had been talking about! I pulled over and stepped out of the car. The spot was filled with power, wild and clean. The ocean waves seemed to toy playfully with the long wall as they slapped against it, as if barely tolerating its presence, as an excuse for not having to deal with the hunks of frozen metal on the other side of the narrow road.

I walked over to the machines and could see they had been there for some time, judging by the corrosion encrusting them. I returned to the wall and prayed, for I knew, as Henry said, that I had gone too far. I hoped that the gods had wanted me to see this place and that I wouldn't be found lacking in some way, so that I would find Auntie Bee.

After praying, I felt centered. I got into the car and slowly drove back the way I came. After about a mile or so,

I noticed the one little road that looked more like it could be a driveway again. I pulled in and, to my astonishment, was almost immediately surrounded by animals; they seemed to come from every direction. A rooster landed on the hood of the car, about four dogs of various sizes were happily barking. Geese, ducks, and chickens flocked around. I proceeded at crawl speed to a little house with a white porch in front. I carefully opened my car door and was greeted not just by dogs as I expected, but by a white Billy goat that baaa'ed at me. I had to laugh out loud when I realized that one of the four dogs that led me in, as Henry had told me, was not a dog at all but a fat little white pig. All these creatures herded me to the front porch of the house where sitting on the top step was a large, impressive gray cat. This kitty looked me over like a grand vizier. Even though this was years before Harry Potter, I thought even then that if that cat had morphed into a person it would not have surprised me. I greeted the cat as I stepped up on the porch. To my relief this Grand Vizier Kitty rubbed approvingly against my legs. I knocked on the screen door, but no one answered.

I cupped my hands around my eyes and looked through the screen door into the house. Again, surprise! The house was much bigger inside than it appeared on the outside. By the look of the furniture, it seemed that time had stood still at somewhere between 1938 and 1948.

'Hello!' I called out. No answer. I turned around. All the animals were gone. I looked around the porch. There was a rocking chair, a porch swing and a wicker chair. I touched the rocker and it felt somehow very owned. I sat on the porch swing and that did not feel right either. I moved to the wicker chair and, like Goldilocks, it felt just right. I sat down and made myself relax. The air was fragrant, and the scene was quite peaceful when a woman's voice called out from inside the house in a loud annoyed tone 'Well! Who is out there!'

Not sure if she was addressing someone or something else, I jumped to my feet and peeked around the door. Standing inside was an elderly woman about my height who looked like a Hawaiian version of my German grandmother, Oma. Just like my Oma, this Hawaiian lady looked like a force to be reckoned with.

'Me... it's me who's here,' I said, coming up to the screen door and hoping that I did not sound too meek.

'Well, Miss Me,' she said giving me the quick once over. 'I said last week and yesterday, NO MORE REPORTERS!' As she shouted, the bun on her head shook with agitation. 'I'll take a broom to you if I have to, but I will give you a chance, since for some odd reason the animals seem to like you.'

I looked around and there they all were again, having somehow quietly snuck up behind me, sitting all around watching attentively. The goat and the cat on the stairs were a bit unnerving.

'Why would you think I was a reporter?' I asked, confused.

The woman continued, eyeing me suspiciously, 'You sure you're not a reporter? You have the look of questions all about you.'

I took a deep breath and said calmly, 'I'm not a reporter. Yes, I do have questions but I'm not a reporter. Maybe that's why the animals like me. It could also be that they know I love all animals. Besides Henry said to tell you that he sent me.'

'Now what would that fool be doing that for?' she said scratching her head. 'He knows I'm so done with talking about presidents and Lindbergh.'

'Lindbergh? As in Charles? The plane guy?' I was very perplexed.

'You really don't know who I am, do you? Then who *are* you looking for?' she asked.

'I'm looking for Auntie Bee, a *kahuna*.'

'Oh…! Well, in that case, *aloha*! I'm Auntie Bee,' she said, smiling broadly while opening the door and stepping outside. 'I thought you were looking for Mrs. Bea.'

'And who's Mrs. Bea?' I ventured, almost afraid to ask.

'Oh, that's me, too,' she answered cheerfully. 'Mrs. Bea is the wife of my dear dead husband Mr. Bea, a good friend of Charles Lindbergh and several presidents. It's all been talked to death.' She reached over to a basket and pulled out two fans, handing one to me. 'Have a seat, dear, and tell me what this is all about.' She waved her hand and the animals retreated to various spots on or around the porch.

'Well, it was Henry who told me how to find you but that wasn't who sent me.' I pulled out my little slip of paper and handed it to her. 'My teacher is Victor Anderson. He is a shaman, witch and *kahuna*. He told me that he's had four lives in Hawaii. The last one being in early Victorian times, before Hawaii was completely stolen. He said that any *kahuna* would recognize his Hawaiian name. Do you?' I asked.

Auntie Bee glanced at the paper 'Yes, I do, and this is quite a claim. Did he tell you anything about it?' she asked, now fanning herself.

'Very little. just that this was his special name and any *kahuna* should know it,' I responded, fanning myself as well.

'Hmmm, very interesting. What do you wish to talk about?'

'For one thing,' I responded, 'Victor, who is such a storyteller himself, said that I should ask for *kahuna*s who know the oldest stories.

'Oh, really!' She sat up vigorously in her seat. 'Then why don't you tell me a story!'

'Ok!' I said brightly, ever happy to launch into telling tales.

Auntie Bee gave me a grunt of approval before settling back into her seat and closing her eyes.

I told her the tales of the *Menehune* that Victor told me. That they were real people and not some little fanciful Hawaiian gnome. I spoke of their travels and how they had touched almost all parts of our ancient world. Perhaps it was because many of them had loved this land best that their spirits returned to rest and play here, when their time as a people was over.

'Still, now and then, a true little person is born somewhere in the world,' I continued, 'a genetic throwback to a wise and crafty people to remind us of ages gone past and the true history of humankind that contained both the very tall people as well as the little people.' I also added that there are elemental spirits and even other worlds, but that was another story.

Auntie Bee opened one eye. 'Now, that's a good story, and you told it very nicely.'

'Thank you, that will make Victor happy,' I replied.

'He taught you well, but he didn't send you here just to talk of stories. Why else are you here?' Auntie Bee asked.

'One reason is to greet and speak to the gods for Victor. We've greeted Pele first...'

'Good girl,' she broke in, smiling. 'Pele does always like to be first. When was that?'

'Yesterday,' I told her.

Auntie Bee chuckled to herself. 'Of course, it was you, then, who woke the old woman up. What else?'

'It's a little hard to explain. For several months, since earlier in the year, I've been having signs and omens. Everything from dreams to repetitive numbers, mostly 11:11. In various ways I feel this heaviness, like we're in an important time for some reason. Victor said that we are at a crossroads and we must speak to the spirits of this earth. We must go before the gods and show that we *do* care about the earth and our future. I've arranged for many people to pray on this all around the earth when Halley's Comet can be seen again. Next, I need to speak to Uli, but

Victor said that I must first swim in her sacred waters.'

'That's a good idea, but first let's speak of a few more things.' Auntie Bee then told me of her husband's long close friendship with the aviator Charles Lindbergh and how his grave was not far from where we sat, by a small old chapel near the sea. She told me her husband had tended the site till he himself died. Then she told me stories of her great grandmother, who pleaded with Pele about a great lava flow, in order to spare a village. The flow had split in two and went around the village, for her sake. She told me of another great *kahuna*, a queen of the people, who tied *ti*-leaves around her bed as she said her prayers during a great eruption, and then told her people to place her bed in front of the incoming lava flow. The queen then proceeded to lie down on her bed and go blissfully to sleep. When she awakened, she found that the lava had turned, flowing around her, toward the sea and away from her and the people, sparing both the Hawaiian *heiau* temple and the church. Auntie Bee told me of the energies of the earth and how man is always seeking to control this power, mostly in the wrong way for the wrong reasons. She spoke of how as a child she had watched as her grandmother, also a *kahuna*, molded cooling lava into the shapes she needed for her work.

'There are few who recognize such things of power, and even fewer who know how to use them,' she advised solemnly.

By this time, the sun was heading toward late afternoon. 'Oh dear,' I sighed. 'Looks like Linda will not get her meat today.'

'Meat? Your friend wants meat?' Auntie Bee pulled out a pocket watch from her apron. 'It's a little late for that. The stores in town will close in ten minutes. From here that's 22 miles away. From the pools, even driving like a crazy person, you'd not make it.'

'I guess Linda will have to survive meatless one day,

though she has threatened to gnaw on my arm.' I laughed.

Auntie Bee raised an eyebrow.

'Yes, she teases me that she had a cannibal life and still is a little savage at heart and proud of it,' I added jokingly.

Getting to her feet, Auntie Bee walked me to the car. 'So, which frightens you more, your strange friend or your strange experiences?' she asked with a wink.

'Oh, definitely some of my friends at times,' I laughed. 'My life is always full of strange experiences; it might get me a little excited but usually it does not frighten me. Like your animal guardians that already might scare the pants off some people,' I said, getting into the car.

'That's their job.' She smiled. 'Are you a good driver?'

'Yes, very good, and I won't drive like a crazy person even to get Linda meat,' I said. 'It was an honor to have met you. *Mahalo* and *aloha*.'

'*Aloha* to you; you will come again one day. Drive steady, keep your eyes open,' Auntie Bee advised in parting.

I waved a last good-bye out the window as I slowly headed back to the road. I looked in the rearview mirror to see all the animals dutifully stopping at the entrance after escorting me down the driveway. Right behind them was Auntie Bee. Was she waving? Her brow seemed furrowed and her hands were moving quickly in gestures I was not familiar with. She seemed to want me to keep going, so I thought perhaps this was a blessing. *How sweet of her*, I said to myself. I looked at the car clock and meter. The pools were a few miles down as I turned right onto the road. If I saw the big rolling hills with the cattle and white fencing, I'd know I'd gone too far. I watched my meter and started to drive down the road. One mile… two miles… when everything around me started to look fuzzy. I suddenly felt very tired and wanted to close my eyes.

'KEEP YOUR EYES OPEN!' I heard Auntie Bee's voice in my head.

My eyes flew open, as the road seemed to wave in front of me. The car felt more like it was floating than being driven. I felt detached from what was happening, and a crazy thought occurred to me. *She's sending me through time or space somehow*, I mused, before shaking my head and mentally kicking myself. *What am I daydreaming about? Pay attention to what you are doing!* I looked down. The mileage meter indicated two miles. I must be right near the pools, no cattle yet. Something loomed up ahead, and I had to slam on the brakes.

The car thudded and shook coming to a stop, and it felt more like it had just landed than stopped. My mouth hung open as I recognized what was directly in front of me. There, standing in all her grace and serenity, stood the statue of the Virgin Mary. I started to shake uncontrollably, not from fear but from shock. I looked at my mileage meter. According to the meter, I had only driven two miles and about four minutes had passed on the clock.

'How did she do this?' I exclaimed aloud.

From the pools it was almost twenty miles to this spot; because the roads are so twisty it takes at least a half hour to 45 minutes to get here. And where was the white fence, the rolling hills, the turnabouts, the cattle? Did I just fly by them?

'Are you OK?' a man's voice asked kindly through my open window.

I jumped in my seat. 'Yes,' I answered quickly, 'but could you please tell me what time it is?'

'It's about 5 to the hour. You better hurry if you want to get anything in town.'

'Thank you. Could you also tell me how long it takes to get to the pools from here?'

'Oh, the locals can do it in about 20 minutes, but I would take it easy. It's about 30 to 40 minutes. I got to run, just wanted to make sure you were OK. You looked a little dazed. Too much sun, maybe? Drink more water.' The man tipped his hat and pedaled off on his bike.

I tried to get out of the car, but my legs were jelly. *Good Lord!* I thought, *the people in town will think I'm high or drunk. On the other hand, Linda will kill me if I don't at least try.* So, once again I opened the car door. I managed to stand up but became very dizzy. I sat back down. I was filled with a sudden joy. I had to tell someone. I also knew that if I didn't leave now, I'd be driving in the dark. I moved the car and pointed it toward the town but somehow, I could not make myself go there. I could see the store down the hill, not far away, but every time I tried to get out of the car, I was all shaky. People came out of the store and I could see they were closing so I turned the car around and dived back into the jungle. I carefully counted twists and turns, saw the cattle and fences. I prayed that Sheriff Henry would be at the turnabout. He was.

Sheriff Henry looked like he was just getting ready to leave. I stopped right by him and explained what had happened.

'Did you get your meat?' he asked.

'No, my legs were shaking too hard,' I answered sheepishly.

He burst out laughing. 'I hope Auntie Bee will be amused and not think she wasted her effort.'

'I'm a little embarrassed, but I also think the point was the experience and the kindness behind it,' I said thoughtfully.

'And the lesson,' added Henry. 'Never forget the lesson.'

We said our *aloha*s and Henry instructed me to go eat some meat myself in the morning.

I then drove into the park to see Linda standing and waiting for me with a little pile next to her and the not quite setting sun lighting up the sky behind her.

'You didn't bring me any meat, did you?' she asked accusingly, her arms crossed in front of her and her eyes cat slits.

'No, Auntie Bee sent me through space or time or both to the town to get you some but only five minutes were left before closing and my legs were jelly and for some strange reason, I couldn't do it.' I felt quite foolish. 'I'm sorry that the experience affected me to the point I could not deal.' I sighed.

'So, a *kahuna* sent you through time to get my meat and you couldn't do it.' She moved suddenly. I thought, *to bite me most likely*! But instead she grabbed me and kept me from keeling over.

'Jesus! You're as white as a sheet.' She sat me back into the car and stepped over to retrieve her bundles. 'Here, something told me to have this ready,' she said. 'Take your clothes off and put it on.'

'What is this? What are we doing?' I asked, still a little dazed.

Linda unwrapped a large beach towel and held it in front of me. 'It's your bathing suit, milady. Put it on because there's a pool you need to be swimming in, like, right now. The hell with my meat! We'll be feasting on breakfast in the morning. Hurry up, the sun is heading toward setting and goddesses don't like to be kept waiting.' Linda grinned like the Cheshire cat.

Part IV

Storms, Protection and Grace

I was like Alice in the wonderland of Hawaii. The after-effects of my meeting with Auntie Bee, the *kahuna*, left me feeling stretched out and somehow taller than I really am. Linda had gone on ahead to the pools to give me a chance to meditate for a few minutes and then munch on a few crackers and cheese that she had given me. Still feeling tall but steadier, I wrapped a towel around my waist and started up the winding path as well. There were not many people at the pool's edge and only Linda was in the water. She waved merrily at me. A typical white American family was just leaving, and I noted that they had left trash behind, mostly beer and Coke bottles. I was staring down at their pile of refuse from, it felt, about three feet above me. It was an odd feeling. Their boy, about ten or eleven years old, who was watching me, jumped to action and scurried back crablike towards the cans.

'It's OK, I'll pick it up, ma'am,' he told me as he looked up at me meekly.

The boy's surprised family called out to him impatiently. I turned and stared at them as if they were unusual creatures behaving boorishly because they knew no better. They stopped talking. The family consisted of two men in their late twenties to early thirties, a woman about the same age, and a very curious and intelligent looking young girl, twelve or thirteen years old at most. One of the men stopped in mid-sentence as he met my cold gaze.

The boy responded, 'Just a sec, dad,' and the girl stepped forward as well. The father grudgingly cocked his head, indicating that the girl was to help her brother. Lickity split, the two children picked up everything, quickly joined their parents, and headed down the path.

Linda swam over to me.

'Well, that was cool,' she beamed. 'Those people have been partying here all day. The kids seemed really nice. The mother appeared neutral, but those guys! Brothers, I think, beer drinking executive potheads. They better not piss off the gods any more than they already have.'

'How so?' I asked.

'Well, either they're real big fans of Huey Lewis and the News or it's the only tape they remembered to bring with them. They must have played it forty times all afternoon. I like the sound but, after about the tenth time, I'm sure even the gods were sick of it. Anyway, I think our fishing boy would be proud of you because you certainly look as if you could pass for a local now.' She paused, giggling. 'I think you spooked those people a bit.'

'Yes, seems that way,' I replied dreamily, as I unwrapped my towel and stepped into the water. It was the perfect rush of warm and cool. I dove under the water. The sun warmed the top layer, and the cool spring water below refreshed my face and cleared my head. I carefully swam around the pool, thinking nothing at first and staying open to whatever images might appear. I flipped over on my back, and floated. In my ears were the hum of the falls and, in the background, the deep underlying roar of the pounding surf. I took in the smell of the salt in the air mixed with blossoms. The sky was an almost glowing blue with the clouds golden from the low sun.

I closed my eyes and, as I floated, images appeared. Hawaiian women were lined up beside the pools, arms extended and chanting. Some of them were dressed in early Victorian clothes and some in traditional clothing. Others wore grass skirts and flowers. From somewhere there came a buzz or humming which I joined in with. I hummed and sang, praying to be cleansed and afforded a clear mind so I could fulfill my purpose here. I praised Uli for her gift of perfect peace and beauty on earth and the magic of Hawaii, especially on this island. My skin felt warm, even though the sun was setting. It was a period of pure bliss and safety, suspended in time and in the arms of Mother Earth and her ocean pools. All too soon a breeze tickled my face and I opened my eyes. Linda was waiting for me quietly and I knew it was time to leave.

'It's going to rain tonight, so I prepared for it as best I could,' Linda remarked as we made our way back to where she had set up camp.

As we picked our way across a field just by the beach, Linda pointed out where the porta-potties were. Not far from these little outhouses, the family I had met by the pools was setting up a large tent. We continued walking to the campsite that Linda had made in a perfectly sheltered spot. She had pitched our tent in a small hollow of shrubs and small trees, between some sand dunes that were a bit higher up from the beach, with the campfire set closely in the adjacent clearing. A modest pile of kindling was already by the stone and sand circle.

Linda grinned, 'I think our ranger would approve.'

I was about to answer when the sound of 'I Want a New Drug' blasted through the warm clear air.

'Oh gods, here they go again,' groaned Linda. 'I moved us over here in the hopes the dunes would dampen the sound. No such luck.'

I looked up at the sky. The clouds were hanging over the ocean trying to decide whether to rain on land or sea.

'Let's have our dinner and if the music is still blaring at night, I'll talk to them,' I offered, feeling confident that this beautiful place would give rise to reason even in the thickest of heads.

Linda had no such illusions.

'If we let them, they'll keep going until two in the morning, unless the wife has the guts to bean them with a frying pan first, but that pleasure will most likely be left to me,' she responded sardonically. 'Believe me, by ten tonight those two guys will be good and toasted by sun and beer and there will be no reasoning with them.'

'Well. You're most likely right,' I agreed.

We prepared and ate our evening meal, then explored the area around us. We had some neighbors not too far away who seemed to be looking for a little peace and quiet themselves. We explored some interesting twisting trees and everywhere we went Huey Lewis and the News followed us there as well. When we came back to our camp darkness had fallen, and the album was on its fifth or sixth run.

'OK, poke me with a fork, I'm done,' I announced finally. 'I'm going to the bathroom and on the way, I'll talk to them.'

The two men were seated in lawn chairs by the fire, drinking beer. The woman and the children were in the tent, huddled around the entranceway. The eleven-year-old boy's eyes were big, and the girl turned to her mother and brother. 'I told you she would come,' she muttered.

'Good evening,' I said in a friendly and even tone to the two men. 'It's become really apparent that you are very dedicated fans of Huey Lewis and the News.'

'And I suppose you have something to say about that?' the father responded. His tone was ugly, and I noted to myself that if it weren't for his attitude and his beer-flushed face, most people would think this joker good-looking.

'Steve!' shouted the woman from the tent. 'Don't make a scene. I told you the kids need to sleep. Shut the damn music off.'

'Look,' said Steve, raising his voice. 'I am from the Bay Area. This is my band, my music. I paid a lot of money for this vacation, and I have the right to enjoy my vacation as I choose.' He emphasized his point by pounding on his beer cooler, eyeing me to see if he'd rattled me.

I had told Linda to stay at camp and that I would handle this myself. Now, in the back of my mind I wondered whether she was lurking, pantherlike, in the darkness. The thought amused me. Unfazed, I answered the drunken sot.

'Well, believe it or not, I'm from the Bay Area as well, and we also paid for our vacation and I too like the band and the album. The bottom line is that you have exercised your right to listen to this album all morning, afternoon, and evening. I am now exercising my right as a fellow camper, and fellow citizen of these here United States with the good people of Hawaii, to inform you that the vacation I paid for was one where we listen to the waves and mediate on the privilege of enjoying such a beautiful sacred place.'

'She means it's her turn,' whispered the boy from the tent.

'Shut the damn thing off,' the woman pleaded again. She's right, Steve. We've all had enough. The children need their sleep anyway.'

'The kids can sleep when they get home! Nobody can tell me what to do in my campsite!' Steve bellowed.

I sighed. 'I asked you nicely. I don't think I'm the only one objecting to your attitude, but I've said my piece.' With that, I turned away, leaving Steve frowning and his friend with a puzzled, half-asleep expression on his face.

After using the outhouse, I crawled into my sleeping bag. I could still hear the strains of 'The Power of Love' on the breeze, by the time my head hit the pillow, and I plunged into a deep, deep sleep.

I woke up to the sound of birds and the need to visit the outhouse. 'I don't want to move,' I protested after seeing Linda dressed and sitting on her sleeping bag with a very happy smile on her face.

'Oh, I think you really need to get up and go pee. On the way, there's quite the sight to see.' She beamed.

'What do you mean?' I asked.

Linda laughed. 'You were so dead to the world last night that you slept through the whole thing.'

'Thing? What thing?' I was scrambling out of my sleeping bag, feeling slightly alarmed at having missed something.

'The storm! A huge storm with thunder, lightning and high winds. And pouring rain,' Linda explained with great satisfaction in her voice. 'This little nook was one of the few safe places. I ran over and helped our neighbors just a few yards away by the trees. I helped them stabilize their tent which was coming down. I tried to wake you up, but you were out cold and looking so snug in your little cocoon, so I took care of things,' Linda finished, with obvious pleasure.

'Gee, I'm glad you had it together. The ocean could have

carried me away and I never would have known! Sorry about that,' I said sheepishly.

'Don't worry at all about it. You were exhausted, and the Gods got busy. Go see while I get breakfast going,' Linda replied, leaving the tent.

I poked my head out. The air was crisp and cool. Raindrops still clung everywhere like small crystals. The sky was overcast and still foggy. I rubbed the sleep from my eyes and headed for the bathrooms, but the sight Linda must have been referring to stopped me short. Stuffed into the front cab of their rented truck, sleeping bags and all, were last night's two children and their weary mother. The wind had scattered the family's belongings everywhere. The men were huddled together like two half-drowned rats. Their tent was wrapped around them like a blanket, and they shivered as they sipped from a thermos that, hopefully, contained coffee. Both men glared up at me.

I took a deep breath and, head held high, walked past them to the outhouse. By the time I returned to our tent, Linda had a fire crackling merrily away, boiling water in our largest pot. We looked at each other and burst out laughing simultaneously.

'If ever, as an adult, there was a time for us to stick our thumbs in our ears and make horns and go "naan, naan, naan, naa, naa", this is it,' Linda chuckled.

'Yeah, I know, but the kids...' My voice drifted.

'That's the only reason I didn't do it already,' Linda snorted. She poured the oatmeal into the pot as I cut up fruit to mix it with trail mix. I was about to add this to the pot when I heard the soft clearing of a throat and there standing nervously at the edge of our campsite, hand in hand, was a damp version of Hansel and Gretel.

'We have visitors,' announced Linda.

'You two look like Hansel and Gretel, if you remember the fairytale,' I told them cheerily.

'Yeah, we remember,' the boy replied, 'and like them,

we're hungry.'

'Well then, you're most certainly welcome,' I said, 'but shouldn't you ask your parents? I don't want them to be angry with you or us.'

'No, it's all right,' the girl cut in. 'We already asked Mom and she knows we're here. Dad and Uncle Rick are busy.'

Linda handed them two steaming bowls of oatmeal and I sprinkled fruit and nuts liberally on top as they sat down. The boy mumbled thanks and shoveled the contents into his face.

Between mouthfuls, he said, 'My dad said you did it. It's all your fault our tents collapsed. He said you're a witch. Is that true? Are you a witch? Did you do it?'

The girl stopped eating and looked at me expectantly. The boy kept munching oatmeal while eyeing me, waiting for my answer. I glanced at Linda, but she too was looking at me with slightly raised eyebrows and an amused look in her eyes, waiting for my response as well.

I took a deep breath. 'I am many different things, and among those things, I could be called a witch because I have pagan beliefs, not just Christian ones. Yet, even though this is part of what I am, I did not curse your father last night. This is a very special place, and I know that both of you can feel that. Your uncle and father, by being unaware and careless, could very easily have offended the spirits of this place.'

'See!' said the girl triumphantly. 'I told you, it's like the commercial said. It's not nice to piss off Mother Nature.'

'We can all say amen to that,' nodded Linda softly and sagely, sipping her coffee.

I cleared my throat. 'Be that as it may, this is the bottom line. Your uncle and dad had been drinking all day, so perhaps they did not tie things down very well. It just so happens that this is Hawaii and it rains here.'

'Not like this,' the boy responded. 'I already asked the

Ranger who came to check on everyone. He said that last night was very strange and unusual for this time of the year.'

'He called it a very odd storm,' the girl added. 'He asked about you guys. We told him that you were in the woods over here someplace.'

'He smiles a lot,' the boy added.

Linda and I glanced at each other.

'Yes. We've noticed that too,' I confirmed, smiling as well.

We could hear someone calling in the distance, and the children leapt to their feet. 'Thanks for breakfast,' the girl said.

The boy nodded his head and grinned. 'We figured if anyone had a warm fire going and breakfast, it would be you guys.'

'Well, you figured right,' Linda replied, smiling at them warmly.

The two children waved merrily as they scrambled off.

'Linda, you knew we'd be feeding them this morning. That's why the big pot.'

Linda grinned as she stamped the fire out while I scooped up sand.

'The kids needed a meal and I figured it would make Uli happy since she was so kind to protect everyone while she taught those jokers a lesson.

'Hopefully they will remember it.' I laughed out loud again. 'The looks on their faces were priceless.'

Part V

The Hand of Uli and the Wild West

We reluctantly left the pools behind and headed back toward what could be called civilization.

'What's next?' Linda inquired.

'We need to find a phone and call Victor,' I replied.

We stopped by an old hotel where there was a pay phone and reported in.

'Where are you now, exactly?' he asked.

We told him where we were the best we could and that we were headed to the airport to hop to another island later that afternoon.

'Hmm.' Victor mused. 'There is a very old sacred spot nearby. The *heiau* may be long gone but you should be able to feel the spot and the energy that runs towards it.'

'You mean like a ley line?' I asked.

'Yes, sort of like that,' he responded. 'It would be nice if you could find the spot and leave an offering there before you leave this island.'

'We have to drop the car off, Victor, so we don't have that much time,' I responded.

'You're doing really well,' Victor reassured. 'Follow your gut, use your instincts. Try to walk the road along the coastline by the airport and see if you can feel it and then follow it toward the water. There should be a road or path there somewhere that will lead you right to it.'

I told Victor that we would try to find it.

We dropped the rental car and our things off at the airport. We were told that the general rule was a ten-minute window wait time and then the plane takes off and we would have to wait till the next day for a plane. I looked at the airport clock. It was barely eleven in the morning and our plane did not leave until ten after four in the afternoon. 'We have lots of time. We can hike along this road here and see if we feel anything. If so, we can follow through with whatever moves us and hike back,' I said, looking at our map.

'Sounds simple enough,' shrugged Linda.

We began walking from the airport. Since the airport was a small one, we were quite soon in the countryside. The sun was bright and warm. We had been walking for quite a while when I felt something odd.

'Hey, did you feel that?' I asked. 'Come up and walk past me, Linda, and tell me what you feel.'

Linda walked by to turn around and walked about 15 feet ahead of me. 'Hmmm. You're right. Something does feels different and odd here, like the gravity changed.'

'Yes,' I agreed. 'It's like we're walking through Jello, starting from about right here.' I took a few steps back to where I felt the change.

'So, I guess this is the spot, but there's no road to the coast here.' Linda looked around as she said this.

'Yes, there is,' I said, pointing.

'That's not a road, that's a driveway,' she protested. 'See, it leads right to that house.'

'And how much you want to bet that it keeps right on going,' I said over my shoulder as I started walking in that direction.

'We still have a plane to catch,' Linda pointed out.

'It's just after one o'clock now.' I replied. 'If we start back at the same pace, we'd be back at the airport around three or so, which leaves us an hour.'

'I would prefer not to cut it too close,' Linda mumbled, eyeing me as she caught up with me, but I was feeling cocky for whatever reason, so bold as brass I marched toward the house.

The house was set back a ways from the road. We

stopped at the front porch; the road wound on behind a barnlike building. I indicated this to Linda.

'That doesn't mean that it keeps going,' she said.

'That's true, and since we are on someone else's property, we should introduce ourselves,' I suggested, walking up the stairs to the porch.

'Hello!' I called into an open screen door. I called out again, and from somewhere in the back of the house, a youngish to middle-aged man with sandy blond hair came towards us with a surprised look on his face. '*Aloha,*' I said, while Linda tipped her hat, 'We were wondering if this driveway is also a road that leads to the ocean.'

'As a matter of fact, it does, but only a few locals know that. What brings you here with all the beaches that are easy to get to?' he inquired.

'We heard there's a very old *heiau* around here, and we were hoping to find it.'

The man looked surprised. 'Again, that's not common knowledge. Not even to all locals.'

Linda looked at her watch. 'We have a plane to catch by 4:10. We were hoping to see the water and honor the *heiau* before we leave.'

The man raised an eyebrow. 'Do you have an offering?' he asked.

It was my turn to be surprised. 'I have some little things with me for that purpose,' I told him.

'Hold on a minute,' he said, moving quickly to the back of the house. He came back with a huge papaya. 'If it feels right, you can put your offerings in this. Or, at the very least, you'll have lunch,' he told us with a warm smile. 'You don't have much time. It's a bumpy and rocky road, just over a quarter mile to the coast. The only people who go there are my neighbors. They fish there. The *heiau* has long fallen apart. But if you hurry and think about what you're doing, you can do this and still catch your plane,' he encouraged. He escorted us out to the road and set us on our way with a smile. We thanked him as he quickly disappeared back inside his house.

The overgrown and rocky road curved before us. 'Why do I get the feeling that this is the yellow brick road and you're Dorothy?' Linda grinned at me.

I laughed. 'And does that make you Toto?' I teased.

'Yeah,' she retorted, 'and I will gnaw on your ankles if you don't start moving down this road.'

At first, the road wound easily through what was mostly ocean grass and underbrush. The sound of insects and birds with the smell of grass and sea hung in the air. Soon the road turned into a four-wheel drive road with ruts and deep potholes.

My trusty wooden sandals protected my feet from the sharp rocks but were not built for speed. Linda, of course, was dressed for any eventuality, and would pass for a dedicated archaeology student. At least my bright yellow dress kept me cool. Both of us were nevertheless relieved when we heard the pounding of surf. The road ended in front of a tall pile of black lava rocks, which at first looked like any beach rock, until when one looked closer. Then one could see some bore the mark and shaping of human hands.

'Well, it looks like this is it,' said Linda, opening her daypack and pulling out the papaya. She pulled out her trusty knife and handed me the fruit along with the knife. I cut into the papaya carefully, inserting the objects that Victor had suggested I bring along.

'This is not going to be easy,' remarked Linda. 'These rocks are hard to climb, and the ocean here is really rough. You have to throw it far out, otherwise the offering will just bounce around in the rocks, where anyone can find it.'

'According to what the man said, not too many people come here,' I replied.

'Maybe not many, but enough.' Linda pointed to the fishing poles set in stones a little ways off. A crumpled beer can glinted in the rocks.

'Well...' I sighed. 'We've come all this way, so here it goes.'

I climbed up on the lava rocks, teetering on my wooden sandals, the rocks being too sharp for bare feet. I slowly made my way a bit further towards the sea, which was a swirling cauldron on the other side of the black wall of piled rocks which, some time ago, must have been a large *heiau*.

Every so often the waves broke through to crash on the rocks on which I was climbing. As the wind whipped my dress and hair about me, I balanced myself and found steady purchase. I held the papaya up high and called out to Uli, intoning a short prayer in Hawaiian that Victor had suggested I use. I opened my heart, closed my eyes, and spoke now plainly in English with whatever came to my mind. I called out to Uli to guide us, so that we might find our way to where we needed to be, for she is mother of the oceans that encircle the world. On opening my eyes again, I saw the ocean swelling towards me; a large wave was going to break on top of me and my first instinct was to run. Such a wave could easily sweep me from my little perch and dash me against the rocks! Yet somehow, I suppressed my fear and threw the papaya in a wide, high arc toward the oncoming water. To my astonishment, the breaking wave reached up and around the offering with what looked so much like a gigantic hand, and pulled itself straight down back into the water with a loud fwap right in front of me. I was sprinkled with only a few drops and a rainbowed mist.

'Did you see that?' I excitedly called out to Linda. 'Wasn't that amazing?

Linda looked slightly shaken having come up a ways, standing on a flat rock.

'Yes, it was, Cornelia. You gave the goddess an offering and she came and got it. But gods! In some way it was scarier than the quake at the volcano. Besides, we're all alone out here and it's five to three. We'll never make it back in time if we don't leave now and even then, maybe not.'

Linda was, thankfully, helping me climb back down because it was harder to keep my balance going downwards. We were standing back on the sand when we heard a plane engine overhead. We both looked up and watched a plane come from high in the sky on the left, over the water and dive in closer and closer till it was over the treetops towards our right, heading in the direction of the airport.

'I have an idea!' I announced excitedly. 'Remember the map and how the airport was placed. The road we followed curved out before curving back towards the coast.'

'Yeah?' Linda responded.

'So, if we cut through the jungle in an angle in that direction, we'll save loads of time.'

'You mean, like follow that plane, and we just dive into the jungle?' Linda responded incredulously.

'Yeah!' I responded, with enthusiasm

'Is this some sort of test? Or are you just crazy and desperate?' Linda asked, in a surprisingly calm tone.

'It's the only crazy thing I can think of that will get us to the plane in time. And maybe it's a test, or maybe another adventure, but I'm willing to go for it if you are,' I encouraged.

Linda relented with resolve. 'Then let's go. You lead.'

I was on the spot and had to come up with a plan of action. Following the rocky coast would take forever and the rocks seemed wilder and harder to climb the further one got from the old *heiau*. My gut told me to head for the fishing lines that were secured in a rocky outcropping on the edge of the jungle above us. I took off my shoes, stepping carefully so as not to cut my feet. Once there, we found the sheltered spot where, I'm sure, many a peaceful afternoon had been spent.

'I don't see a path anywhere,' Linda remarked.

'I do.' I pointed towards a little path about six inches wide that led into the shrubbery.

Linda wrinkled her nose. 'That's an animal path, like water rats or a mongoose, or something.'

'Yes, but that's all there is. So, let's look.' I parted the greenery and stepped through.

The temperature was cooler in the jungle. A thick blanket of low-lying plants covered the ground. Palms and various other trees towered above us. After a short distance the path split in two. One path curved towards the road we had come in on, and the other, smaller path headed in the direction that the plane had gone.

'Well, that's the path people use now and then, and this is where the critters go.'

'Oh, great,' Linda moaned. 'We're going to follow some barely existent path to some unnamed creature's burrow in the middle of nowhere.'

'Think about it, Linda,' I answered, as I pulled the back part of my dress forward between my legs and hooked it into the front of my bra, turning it into a huge diaper – silly looking but practical, I thought. 'Why would small animals come to the ocean?'

'Maybe hunting for crabs. It certainly would not be for water,' Linda replied.

'True. They're looking for food, maybe crabs, but the path came out at the human campsite, so maybe the animals are scavenging for what people leave behind. The man who gave us the papaya indicated that his neighbors lived on the other side of the road, and it should be possible that these little critters are going to head towards the only other place nearby where humans might leave trash, like airport dumpsters.'

Linda was amused. 'You know, you're scary when you

make sense.'

'Thanks, I guess,' I replied dryly.

Soon we were walking through the undergrowth. It was like stalking through salad when my sandal slipped off.

'What about snakes?' Linda asked with some concern, as I poked about for the sandal.

'I don't believe Hawaii has snakes,' I answered with a little whew to myself as I retrieved my sandal, slipping it back on and resuming my stalk through the underbrush. 'I figure that if we walk as quickly as we can, we won't have time to pay attention to any crawly thing we might find disturbing.'

'Hmm. I'll try to remember that if I ever hike the Amazon.' Linda laughed. 'By the way, do you think that guy back there was some kind of *kahuna*? I mean, he really helped us, even gave us an offering. For a regular looking white guy with a tan that was pretty cool.'

'Yes, he was,' I agreed. 'Still, I don't think he was a *kahuna*. I didn't feel moved to show him Victor's paper, but he obviously is a spiritual person who knows the area very well.'

The buzz of another small plane filled the sky above us.

'Yes, we're heading in the right direction.' I was both determined and relieved, picking up the pace and following the sound.

'Oh, my God!' announced Linda, 'It's ten to four. We'll never make it if the plane is on time.'

No sooner were the words out of her mouth than we stumbled out into bright sunlight. Airport runways stretched out before us. The little plane had taxied to a stop by the small airport building where we had left our belongings.

'Well, there's only one thing left to do,' I said, taking off my sandals. I untucked my dress from my bra and gathered it up in one hand so I would not fall over it. 'Remember to look both ways!' I called out as we dashed across the runways, running as fast as we could.

We arrived at the front desk bedraggled and panting. Three stony faces were there to greet us. 'What the hell do you think you guys were doing?' said a big, heavyset Hawaiian man.

'It's only five after four. Our plane should not have left yet. I know we cut it a little close,' I said apologetically.

'Close? Cutting it close? That's what you think this is about?' he bellowed. 'It's about this,' he said as he turned his desk monitor around to show us a security video of Linda and I emerging from the jungle to dash madly across the runways. Linda was holding onto her hat, I was holding up my dress, sandals in my other hand with my long hair flying behind me.

'We looked both ways before running across,' I offered sheepishly.

'They looked both ways before crossing.' The Hawaiian man turned toward his coworkers and continued sarcastically, 'Now, isn't that thoughtful?' He was tall, big and quite intimidating and now snapped his head around to me with a big glare to ask 'Are you trying be cute here? Have you any idea how many laws you've broken? I'm supposed to arrest you!' He was getting redder under his brown skin with every breath. I just wanted to sink through the floor.

'Do you know how much trouble this airport could be in if I don't report you?' He was almost shouting. 'In all my years of working here, no one has ever come running out of the jungle to catch a plane. What would you have done if it had been a few minutes later and the plane was taking off? Run and tackle it down, maybe hang on to the wings! Hmmm... Last we saw you two, you were out that front door walking down the road.' He pointed.

'Well, we walked a lot further than we planned, and we wanted to see the water one more time and... (at this point, I thought better of trying to explain the *heiau*) ...so we headed towards the coast. It got late, and we were desperate, so we cut through the jungle. I didn't think about the runways and had no idea it was illegal to cross them,' I explained in my most sincere tone and added again, 'and we did look both ways before running across.'

'Have you ever heard that ignorance of the law is no excuse?' he replied in a very serious tone.

'Yes, in the Wild West, like in old cowboy westerns,' I answered meekly.

'Well, Hawaii is as far west as you can get now, isn't it?' He grinned.

My heart was about to sink to my knees when one of the women quietly announced, 'Their plane is ready.'

'Well,' mused the big man, 'you know what they did in the old west with unwanted criminals?'

'Didn't they hang them?' asked Linda with raised eyebrows.

'That was always an option back then.' He smiled, showing all his square white teeth. 'But usually no. They just told them to get the hell out of Dodge. So, get on your plane, please,' he said, with emphasis on the please with a stiff smile. 'And if you go to another island before heading home, please don't pull any more stunts that will upset the locals. Have a good flight and *aloha*,' he added in a flat tone.

Linda grabbed the boarding passes and my arm at the same time. 'Let's make tracks,' she whispered.

Once settled on the plane, I let out a big sigh of relief. 'You know what I'm afraid of, Linda?'

'What?'

'That tape they have of us running across the runways is going to end up in some archive and it will end up being a training film for years to come for park rangers and airport personnel as to what crazy things mainlanders do.'

'Would not surprise me in the least,' agreed Linda as she put on her seat belt, while I rummaged in my purse, pulling out a brush and lipstick.

Linda now looked at me with total amusement. 'How can you talk to a *kahuna*, traipse through a jungle, become a criminal, and still be such a girl?' She laughed. 'You are such a nut.'

'Well, as Victor would say, better to be a nut than be off your nut,' I retorted, putting on lip-gloss.

'I'll have to talk to him about that one someday,' laughed Linda. 'So now, what's next?'

'Lono. The God Lono. Other than that, once we find him, I have no idea.' I relaxed back in my seat and looked out the window as our little plane skipped like a dragonfly over the blue, blue water.

Part VI

The Search for Lono

Once we reached Kauai, We were not sure where to start.. We'd been given the name of a family. They were friends of my husband and were kind enough to offer us a place to stay. We'd asked for a map at a gas station , but the station had run out of them, so we decided just to drive around for a while. After all, one could drive from one end of Kauai to the other in less than a day. Getting the lay of the land would certainly not be a waste of time.

As we drove through the breathtaking scenery, we could not help but notice little white signs announcing this camp and that kind of camp.

'Well, they certainly have a lot of camps on this island,' I mused to Linda.

'Yep,' she answered. 'Have you noticed what kind of camps they are?'

'No,' I said. 'I'm driving and it's flashing by a little fast. A lot of them look like Bible camps, though.'

'How about all of them?' stated Linda, while digging around for something to nibble on.

'You're kidding! Aren't some KOA camps or clubs of some kind?' I replied.

'Nope,' she responded. 'Maybe off the road, but by these signs so far not a single one. I've seen just about every denomination out there and a few I've never heard of.' Linda grinned at me as she spoke.

'Hmmm... Maybe this is the island where all the local churches have their getaway spot. After all, didn't Victor tell us that Christianity is now also deeply imbedded in the Hawaiian psyche?'

'Nice thought, sweetie,' answered Linda dryly, 'but I think this is where all the different churches from the mainland have their vacation bible school spots.'

'But why here? The other islands have much more room,' I asked curiously, slowing the car to a stop.

'Maybe because it's out of the way,' Linda surmised. 'Even though this island is famous for its beauty it's not as common a tourist spot as some of the other islands. Besides, it's all very impressive. God's handiwork and all that. Why are we stopping, by the way?'

'See that young woman over there and the bar across the street?' I indicated with my head. 'I just saw out of the corner of my eye some really local looking guys walk into the place, so they should know this address we're searching for. Otherwise, the young woman looks pretty local to me, and I bet that tiny little *lei* shop is hers or she works there. I'll go over there to ask her some questions if I can't get anything out of the guys.'

'Are you sure you don't want me to go with you?' asked Linda with raised eyebrows.

'Naw, I'll be fine. Stay here and watch the car and I'll be right back,' I said over my shoulder.

'Hey!' called out Linda. 'What do I do if you dazzle the locals with that smile of yours? Do I just hang out here while you chit chat forever?'

'Don't worry. If I bedazzle anyone, I'll lead them out here to you like the Pied Piper.' I winked.

'Right,' droned Linda with a roll of her eyes. 'Time to get comfortable' With that, she bounced up on the hood of the car and lay down, pulling her hat over her eyes.

It was curiosity that made me go to the bar first. By the looks of it, the place was most certainly a local watering hole. It was cool and dark inside, with the smell of both fresh and stale cigarettes in the air. As my eyes adjusted to the dim light, I realized that the bar was full of men and only men. There were big Hawaiian men, some Filipinos, and Japanese/Portuguese looking men. Most appeared middle aged and scrappy, obviously this area's standard working men.

Both young and old wrapped themselves around their drinks. The vibe was so depressing and bitter that I was frozen to the spot for a moment.

'Well, lady? Are you looking for someone?' asked the bartender in a state-your-business tone of voice.

'Yeah, me!' called a drunken voice from the back of the room. Everyone laughed.

'I'm just trying to find an address around here. This looked very local, so I thought I'd give it a shot,' I explained.

'Yeah, you're right about that, but I wouldn't go looking for any directions from here,' the bartender replied sardonically. 'Go ask the lady that sits in the little house at the corner making *leis*. She gives directions all the time.'

As if on cue, everyone turned their backs and returned to their drinks. I muttered my thanks, slipped out into the bright sunshine, and walked back to the car.

'That was fast,' said Linda, opening one eye.

'You can keep your hat on and keep relaxing. I'm going across the street. It was not a very talkative bar for some reason.' I headed toward the said young woman.

As I got closer to her miniature house, I took notice of its Gingerbread Victorian style. The front porch had just enough room to sit on and display flower and shell *leis* as well. The young woman was wearing a long white lacy dress, Hawaiian style. She was striking, pretty and a bit heavier set, as were some Hawaiians or Native Americans. Her skin was fair, and she had thick hair that was very black and shiny. Her eyes were deep blue. A Hawaiian Snow White, I could not help but think to myself.

I greeted her. '*Aloha.*'

'Same to you,' she responded with a broad smile. I was

invited to sit down on the porch with her. Soon we were talking like old friends. I quickly found out that she, like others we'd met, had interesting tales to tell. She spoke easily of her Native American and Irish background. One of her relatives had been stationed to the Islands during World War II and fell so much in love with the land and culture that he returned to Hawaii after the war. The young woman's family now lived part time on the islands and the rest of the year on the mainland. She sold *leis* to the tourists and made Native American style jewelry for the locals, who really admired and collected her pieces. She also informed me that the bar across the street did service the local workers, but there tended to be a lot of bad attitude there.

'Why?' I asked, 'It's so beautiful here.'

She explained that there was a lot of bitterness. 'First there are only a few true Hawaiians left on this island, with the few of the mixed Hawaiians that are of the old royal and old missionary family lines. There are also very mixed Hawaiians of old families, along with families of other races who have been there a long time, such as some Chinese families, for example. Then there are those more modern Hawaiians who have little or no Hawaiian blood but have been on the islands since the Second World War or, at the very least, since the Sixties. Now, there is a new influx of rich people from all over, competing with each other to buy a piece of paradise. All this, not to mention all the corporations and churches that have camps and condos galore here. This island is like a lost jewel to some,' she continued. 'That's why many of the locals of pure blood or nearly pure blood have moved to the forbidden island. Once there, they feel that they can at least live with dignity following as much of the old ways as possible, and not be a tourist attraction for every *haoli* (mainland white people) that comes along.'

It sounded like a good solution on the surface, but from

what she'd heard, life on the forbidden island involved a challenging lifestyle that required adjusting to.

'The forbidden island is not like others with valleys, forests, and microclimates. It's smaller and dryer than it is here, but they do have seashells that are found nowhere else in the world,' she continued, reaching down and showing me some small white and pearlescent shells. She'd accepted the shells in trade for *leis*, for such flowers are not as easily found on the forbidden island.

She also informed me that she managed to keep herself connected to all her traditions by her art, which included traditional Irish and Native American styles and to the Hawaiian styles by her flower *lei* creations. The local people saw her as being genuinely tribal and akin to their ways. I was shown the little room behind the porch where she stored most of her things; the native jewelry and even Christian crosses which she takes home every night.

'I was broken into once,' she said with a small smile. 'I don't think it will ever happen again.'

'So, you feel protected?' I asked

'Don't you?' she shot back; eyebrows raised.

'Yes, because my friend and I honored Pele at her volcano on another Island and certainly since then things have felt directed,' I responded

'Well, you can honor her here as well. There's a volcano but the only way to get to it easily is by helicopter. After a slight pause, she continued, 'Some say that this is where Pele first rose from the waters and started her walk. I tend to think she'd been walking here already for a long time.'

We both laughed.

'Right now, we're looking for Lono. Any ideas?' I inquired.

'I guess it's all in how you look at it,' she answered. 'It's said that Oahu is Lono's island, but if his sign really is the cross, then here in Kauai is a good place for him to be.' She followed this statement with a chuckle.

'I don't understand,' I replied as I watched Linda, somewhat in the distance, stretch, slowly peel herself off the hood of the car, and begin ambling toward us.

'Lono is a god of music and the growth of all plants. He is also one of the four great gods. He brought gifts to mankind. He gave us games, music and easier ways to grow food. He is thunder and rain. His energy and power are in the lightning. The gift of his healing is in the rainbow. It is said that he left the islands and promised to return one day.'

'Wow... he sounds a lot like Quetzalcoatl of the Mexican Indians,' I remarked.

'The Hawaiians feel akin to many tribal people around the world. Even the Jews were once tribal if you think about it or bother to read ancient history.'

'So, are you telling me that Jesus is Lono because in Mexico there are those who feel that Quetzalcoatl was Jesus as well? Are there Mormons here?' I wondered aloud.

'As I said before, everyone is here,' said Linda, joining the conversation.

'This is my friend Linda, who I'm traveling with and this is...' I paused when I realized I did not know her actual name.

'Angela,' she quickly stated. 'Nice to meet you, and you have me curious. Why are you so interested in Hawaii's old gods?'

'We're on a quest of sorts. I have a friend back in the Bay Area, Victor, who is both shaman and *kahuna*. He wants me to connect with and, speak with Pele, Uli, and Lono. There is so much we still don't know, such as why those three gods are special, for example. I had no idea that there were so many gods in Hawaii, let alone how they related to each other. Victor called Uli Pele's sister but, according to the prayer he gave me, she is also the Great Mother.'

Angela replied quite thoughtfully, 'Well... depending

on what kind of *kahuna* he is and how he's related to the gods, any *kahuna* can call upon the gods as sister, brother, mother, father, depending on their connection and/or the manner in which he's appealing to them. The same is true of the gods themselves. Relationships that we think of in human terms are thought of a little differently here. Also, those three gods are very protective. A *kahuna* would only call upon them together for healing or protection, even mercy, on a pretty big scale.'

'Why do you say that?' I asked.

'Not all the Hawaiian gods care about people. Some may care about a certain island, area, tribe or family but not about humankind in general. On the other hand, those three gods do seem to care about the fate of humanity.'

'I did not realize that. You've given me a lot to think about. And all I thought I was doing was coming over to ask you if you knew the whereabouts of this address.' I handed her the piece of paper with the address of our next contact on it.

Angela glanced at the paper. 'Oh, I know where this is,' she said, quickly scribbling a little map on the back and returning it to me. 'You know,' she remarked as she did so, 'this is a good place, but like you saw in the bar it also has its embittered people. It has its underbelly, so be careful in your quest and how you speak to people. It's not always wise or safe to be frank.'

Shortly thereafter we warmly took our leave from Angela. Nevertheless, I observed a warning in her eyes and took it seriously as we said goodbye.

Using Angela's map, it did not take us long to find the house we were looking for. It was beautiful, and we discovered that Robert had built it himself for his wife Sara and their child Lori. Linda and I told Robert's family how kind it was of them to invite us to share their company despite not knowing us personally. We were assured that such was all within the *aloha* spirit. All of us sat down with cool drinks and were told more about Robert and his family. Robert was a carpenter and Sara a Bible School teacher. They spoke of their love for their island and of its limitations.

Nevertheless, Robert and Angela told us;

'We're really concerned about Lori's happiness and education as she approaches her teen years. She's one of a small handful of white children on the island that live here the year round. We've been thinking of moving to a bigger island, or even to the mainland.'

Linda responded to this with some surprise in her voice. 'I thought that Hawaii is famous for its open-heartedness and interracial marriage.'

'Yes, that's true on one hand but on the other, it's not,' so simple Robert replied. 'You see, there was a time when everyone, no matter who they were – white missionaries, businesspeople, Chinese workers, etc. – had a purpose for being here, whether they were sugar cane workers or cowboys for the cattle ranches. Now, in today's modern life, people's roles are not so clear-cut, and everyone desires the modern conveniences that come at a price. It's hard to make big money on an island, even considering the tourist trade. So, there's a lot of competition and that comes with its own problems, such as gangs, drugs, and everyone wanting their own territory. Sure, there's still quite a bit of the *aloha* spirit here, but it must stand in the face of those modern demands and issues. It's understandable how the full natives and the ones who have been here for many generations have very mixed feelings, let alone resentment, for the good and bad that tourism has brought here.'

While Robert spoke, my eyes drifted over to a wall behind a small table with flowers on it. On the wall was a very attractive grass weaving in the shape of a cross.

'What is that on your wall?' I asked. 'It's quite pretty'

Sara smiled broadly. 'That's Hawaii's hope. That is the cross of Lono, a Hawaiian god and protector of many good things, like the fertility of the earth and the health and plenty of the oceans. He's also the harbinger of music and dance, as he came to Hawaii bringing rainbows, following his rain and thunder. Hawaiian legends say that he slid to earth on a great rainbow when he came here.'

I gave Linda a meaningful look as she got up and walked to the wall to get a closer look at the cross. 'We've been hearing about this lately,' she said.

'We've heard that some people feel that Lono may be Jesus,' I added.

'Well... It's all very poetic thinking,' said Robert with a small sigh. 'We like to think of it that way, as many locals do, because we're Christian. When we first came here, we were just hippie runaways. Then we accepted Jesus into our hearts. Now we live a simple but godly life and are very happy. How about you folks?' he asked.

Linda spoke first. 'My mother is Muslim, and my father is Jewish, so I don't do the Jesus thing. In other words, I think that he set a good example to follow as a person, but to worship him as God, well, my mom and dad would see it as bad form, you know.'

I was very proud of Linda. She got that out with no sarcasm and a minimum squirm factor. Then all eyes turned to me.

I cleared my throat. 'I was raised Lutheran. The ecumenical Jesus movement was very popular in my college. I'm secure in what I know and feel to be true, for the part of me that was raised Christian. But I also honor other parts of my heritage and feel truth there as well...'

Before Linda or I could say anything else, Sara broke in: 'Well, then, you're invited to our church evening beach supper. It may be a little clouded over, but we'll pray that the Lord will provide.' With this statement, Sara raised her hands and we joined together in a circle around the table. Sara thanked God for our safe journey and asked Him if we could enjoy our picnic without rain. With that, Linda and I helped the family gather food to put in the cars.

We drove to a lovely little beach. Next to it was a very simple structure that belonged to the church and was used for Bible School and prayer meetings. There, Linda and I were greeted warmly, and soon the beach was bustling with activity. Many children played here and there, their faces and arms glowing with the tones of various cultures and the kiss of the Hawaiian sun. The clouds were dark with rain and a slightly cool but comfortable breeze was blowing over us. The children gathered large rocks to hold down the tablecloths, while the men made a crackling fire. A large barbecue began. Linda took our car to get some extra coals from the store. As she did this, I wandered towards the ocean. There the coastal breeze was pushing the rain clouds out to sea, exposing the brilliant blue of the sky. It was at that moment, and within an eye blink, that not just one or two or even three rainbows appeared, but five of them. Each arched like bridges of light from one mountain peak to another.

'Oh, look!' I cried out, 'Look at all the rainbows!'

'Yes, that's the gift of Lono, as we say here,' answered a small woman walking towards me. Other people smiled indulgently at me.

'I guess you must have multiple rainbows here a lot and I'm just betraying what a mainlander I am by being so excited,' I confessed, slightly embarrassed by my own enthusiasm.

'Yes, we do, but this isn't something we take for granted. To see any rainbow is always a blessing.' The small woman said kindly. 'Whether you are Hawaiian or *haoli*, it's still Lono's and God's promise to humankind.'

'So, you feel, like many Mexican Catholics and others, that the Pagan old ways and Christian ways can live side by side?' I asked.

She paused thoughtfully for a moment before speaking. 'One set of my grandparents came from the Philippines. We were already a mixed people there. In my family there, we have some Spanish and Chinese, and for others here, it's Portuguese and Polynesian, now mixed in with the many different peoples on our islands. At home I have a special place where I remember and honor my ancestors, as they would have wished, but I do not worship them. On my mother's side, there's Hawaiian, Portuguese and even a little white. Look at my children. Are they not the promise of the future, especially if we open their eyes to God's word to love and be honorable to one another?' she asked, in a sincere and kindly fashion.

I looked at her before responding in just as sincere and kindly a tone, 'Don't you believe that all the cultures throughout all of time, each in their own way, have tried to live a good life? Have they not loved their children too? Have not the gods of India and the Native Americans encouraged their people to live moral lives just as much as the ones from the Middle East?' I continued 'After all, the laws of God are written on all men's hearts, as Paul told us in the Bible.'

'It's only in Christianity that God sacrificed himself for all humankind and promised to return, and it's only in Christ that we can accept ourselves and all others in his perfect love,' she returned in a manner that brooked no dissent.

'Well,' I smiled. 'Your children are beautiful, it did not rain, the rainbows appeared and the food smells great, so we are indeed blessed by God and Lono and that is for sure.' We both laughed and headed back. The smell of food now hung in the air, making our mouths water.

Later in the day, we went to another lovely little beach with only a few children playing in the tidepools. We came back for dinner and to pitch our tent in the back yard at the house in which we were staying. After dinner Robert told us where to go to find various tourist services in the morning which interested Linda. He also spread out a map giving us the lay of the land. There was a dry side of the island and a wet one. Even though we were on a mission this was the island on which Linda wanted to be more of a tourist. We would just keep our eyes open to whatever signs might present themselves.

The next day, we drove at a leisurely pace through the countryside and small towns until the road turned inward and the land became more arid.

To our amazement, we found ourselves at the mouth of a great canyon. Truly a smaller version of the Grand Canyon in the mainland. We walked for a while with some tourists, listening to a park ranger explaining the history of this part of the island. He pointed out to us the wild goats climbing the cliffs in the distance. It is usually wild pig that is common fare for a *luau*, a festive Hawaiian, usually dinner-type feast, with *hula* dancing, that the hotels put on for tourists, but it is still a part of traditional Hawaiian life. Goat meat can be part of this fare as well. We took the short walk and took some photos and returned to the car.

We found another local café that served every kind of way spam could be served. We ended up eating big fat waffles with macadamia nuts, pineapple syrup and a side of spam. Not bad at all. We drove and stopped frequently to take pictures of the land, such as the *taro* fields and what looked like an abandoned sugar mill. We explored one small town to see how locals went about their business. Many were working their fields and ranches. We needed to be careful as people crossed from field to field while huge trucks hauled out cut sugar cane. As the twilight came, we headed for our local home. The moon was now visible. There was no traffic, and we drove in no hurry. All was still around us, so we were quite startled when an owl flew right up the hood of the car making me slam on the breaks. It flew out over a tall sugar cane field. Our car was right by its entrance.

'Well, shall we follow that bird?' asked Linda

'Didn't someone say that it is not a good idea to drive around in sugarcane fields, that you could get lost?' I answered.

'Yeah, I think there was mention of that somewhere, but I feel like having an adventure,' chuckled Linda, grabbing her hat from the back seat.

'Well, as they say, be careful what you ask for.'

We dove in. The sugar cane was very high, so this was a field either ready for harvest or left up for tourists. The bumpy road seemed to be set up like a square spiral taking us deeper into the cane. I did not want to get stuck here, so I raced along at a good clip taking turn after turn. 'We have no idea how big this field is' I remarked to Linda as I turned on the lights, for it was now fully dark.

'No, we don't but we're on an island, so it can't be that big,' she responded brightly.

Before I could get much more concerned, we broke into a large open space that had more than one entrance. I brought the car to a stop and turned off the lights. 'Roll up the windows,' I stated.

'Why? There's no one around.'

'We kicked up a lot of dust,' I offered as an explanation

but deep down I thought it was a better idea to have the windows shut if we had to jump back in the car for any reason. From the car the tall canes looked a little creepy.

We got out of the car and gazed up into the sky. We were still inland, so it was deeply silent, no crickets, with a bright moon shining and the sparkle of diamond stars. It was beautiful and awesome. I could not help but think as I stood there how the early Hawaiians, or any of our ancient ancestors, must have felt confronted by the heavens at night. *Deep, silent and bright is thy mystery* were the words that came to mind. I thought of the people of these islands, their culture and way of life. How it had all changed and how just like the Native Americans there was so much death brought in by disease and by the violence of modern weapons and drugs. I thought about Victor's love for island culture and the respect he had for their connection to the earth and the spirit world. Is humankind really advancing? Are we really bothering to pay attention at all? I took a deep breath and thought of how busy we are, almost like ants. We think of ants as annoying, so we brush them away and kill them, sometimes by the thousands, because they are building their homes where they should not – according to us. Instead of advancing in heart and spirit, have we instead become hyper focused on just becoming like ants, always building more: more people, more buildings, more goods, more power over others, with no thought either for the bigger picture of the present or for the future? Emotionally we have duty, loyalty and devotion to our flag, religious beliefs, businesses. Even the most evil and notorious criminals and gangs of the world have such fealty, although some might see it more as discipline. What about the refinement of caring and love and all its expressions in music, art and life itself? Nature is the divine artist, yet are we not her hands too? What about that power? What about that love? Is this not the key?

'Hey, check that out.' Linda broke into my thoughts.

I turned to look into the middle of our enclosure and there floating at waist height were long wispy clouds of fog. They shimmered in the night air giving a quite ghostly effect. The temperature had dropped enough to give a light chill to the air.

'We should get going. The fog might get thicker,' I cautioned.

We got into our car and, after talking about it, decided to take the exit that we had come out of, turning back hopefully out. As we started spiraling back, we were confronted with thickening clouds of fog. Not only was this quite spooky, but it made it harder to see, and after a while we found ourselves back where we started.

'Hmm, I didn't think we turned back at any point, unless we've ended up in some sort of time warp,' Linda mused casually, which made me laugh.

'If we keep driving in circles we'll run out of gas and it will get pretty cold with this fog tonight. So, the good point of being back here is that we know our starting point and we just have to make sure we are turning out not in.'

'How are we going to be able to tell? Just keep turning right?'

'This is a square spiral so every fourth one might do it.'

'Sounds like a plan. Let's do it!' Linda sounded determined.

I hesitated. 'I know maybe this might sound silly but what also might help is with each turn we visualize ourselves getting out of the maze We should also ask the spirits to please help us out, because we are not drunk, silly people trying to cause trouble.'

'Well, the spirit and energy of the land has to put up with people all day, so them wanting the night for themselves would not surprise me. We meant no harm or disrespect, so they should help us out,' Linda said with confidence.

I drove our car now at a slow steady pace. In the back of my mind I thought of Hawaiian ghost stories and could see how easy it would be to conjure one up, but I kept this thought to myself as we counted our turns, and instead prayed under my breath. When we popped out, it was like a little shock. The moon lit the road and there was mysteriously no fog anywhere. With thankful hearts we got back on our way.

Part VII

Courage in the Light and Dark

The next day we visited a hotel lobby that Robert told us was full of brochures announcing all kinds of tours that tourists could take. Linda snatched up the one that offered helicopter rides.

'Yes, totally cool!' she beamed. 'The two things that I really want to do here, scuba dive and helicopter ride.'

'Really, Linda, are you sure you can afford this, because I know I can't. Frankly I feel a little nervous about this for some reason,' I told her honestly.

'Look, I don't care what it costs,' she burst out. 'I saved for myself and a friend. I've let you and the gods drag me all over these islands and now I want to have some tourist fun for a hot minute, and I don't care what anybody or anything has to say about it.' Linda crossed her arms and frowned at me. Such was about as close to a defiant pout that she could get.

I sighed. Linda had been such a good sport and I knew from the beginning that this was something she really wanted to do. I reached up and touched my Native American pin that I had been wearing throughout our journey. I thought about how Victor had said that we were being protected and guided and how this was also Linda's vacation before answering.

'Of course, you should do this. it's just I've never scuba-dived before and that puts limitations on where they can take us. You're experienced, and you should go have fun without me holding you back, and you'll save a little money besides,' I reasoned.

'Yes, yes, oh wise one. Your logic is perfect as usual,

except for one thing. I don't give a flying fart in hell if we are in a kiddy tide pool or out in the middle of the ocean,' she said flatly.

'Well, then, I guess we're going scuba diving.' I replied.

A big grin spread across Linda's face.

Of those we contacted, there was only one outfit that was willing to take us as is; in other words, to supply gear and take on a person who had never dived before. All the others wanted to charge extra to give me two hours' training in a pool first. This, of course, sounded like a good idea, but we were, after all, trying to save some money. So, we drove up to the office of the "as is" outfit and walked in. We were greeted by what the girls of our day would call a god. I would say a godling, at the very least.

When this godling stood up, he was at least six-foot, three. He was wearing a blue and aqua swimsuit that complimented his remarkable green-blue eyes. From his perfectly cut, longish blond hair, to perfect teeth and long elegant hands, there was not one inch of this Apollo that was imperfect. We somehow managed to speak coherently as he explained in a professional manner how and where we were going to dive. He answered my questions and showed me how to put on the mask and how to breathe with it. He assured me that all was safe and, since this was my first time, someone would be with me the whole time and walk me through it.

He, on the other hand, would personally take Linda out to some reefs where she could look at some interesting things since she was an experienced diver. He asked Linda if she had any limitations. She told him with no hesitation that she really, really does not like sharks and that she even hates looking at them in an aquarium.

'Not all sharks are dangerous, you know, and you are in the ocean, after all,' he responded evenly.

'I know that!' laughed Linda. 'I'm not going to be

unreasonable about it or anything. It would just be very cool if sharks could be avoided. And don't worry, if we do see one, I won't freak out on you,' she added.

The next thing we knew, we were in an open-air jeep heading toward the beach. Linda and I were accompanied by three young men of various ages. We sat in the back with two of them, both smiling at us. We decided that the best course of action was to make small talk by asking how long they had been in the scuba diving business.

'Oh, nearly two years. We took over from the guy who had it before. You know, I could not help but notice the pin you're wearing. It's really unusual,' said the slightly older of the two facing us. I noted that he was trying to sound very neutral.

'Well, here it's unusual because it's American Indian, but on the mainland, people would generally recognize it as being Native American,' I responded, in as friendly and casual manner as I could.

'Oh, I see,' he said.

The older guy and his friend looked at one another and then he proceeded to continue with his questions.

'I was just thinking that it reminds me of some Hawaiian statues of gods. I thought maybe it was an amulet and that you had some sort of superstition about it.'

Now, I knew exactly where this was heading, and I reacted accordingly;

'One does not think of objects relating to one's personal faith or cultural background as objects of superstition. That's ignorant at best and certainly impolite at worst. I see you're wearing a cross around your neck. Does that make you superstitious?' I challenged.

'Whoa… down, girl' whispered Linda under her breath.

The other young man jumped in without mincing any words: 'So, you're not saved, then?' he asked.

I knew then that there was almost no way of getting out of this whether I said I was or wasn't.

I also realized that I did not want to get into an argument that would ruin Linda's experience because of these two young men. They were most likely just two Christian white boys doing their godly duty.

'Look, I'm sorry for getting a little testy here, but isn't there enough prejudice in this world over skin color, politics and money that we really don't need to throw something as beautiful and personal as religion into that barrel of bad apples?' I pleaded.

'Oh, I didn't mean to get heavy either.' He smiled. 'But you need to understand that when you are saved, you're so filled with God's love that you care about everyone's soul and their salvation, just as God does. So, I feel compelled by the Lord to offer you the gift of Christ.' He turned toward Linda. 'How about you? Have you ever considered Jesus? Are you saved?' he asked her, his voice full of trained sincerity.

'Hey, don't look at me,' answered Linda with a shrug. 'My father is Jewish and my mother's Muslim.'

'What did she say?' asked the driver who up to this point had said nothing.

'She said her father's Jewish and her mother is Muslim,' called the young man over his shoulder.

'Oh,' was the reply. The three of them exchanged glances and apparently, they must have decided that Linda was beyond saving so they returned their attention to me.

'Your skin color is much too white to be an Indian and you certainly don't talk like one so what are you, anyway?' asked the young man who had been doing most of the talking.

'Good Lord!' My eyes flew wide open. 'I can't believe you guys. Native Americans come in all shades from dark coppery brown to quite fair and what makes you think you know what Indians talk like? You think it's like the movies or something? Me want to be speaking to your white chief. You gotta be kidding me! My skin is fair, but my heart is dark like a deep forest, and you should be taking that into consideration before saying any more hurtful things!' I was by now quite distressed, and thankfully we had arrived at a lovely beach area so nothing more was said. We drove right up to Mr. Apollo who was already there with all the gear.

'Here're your wetsuits,' he offered and pointed toward a couple of small shacks where we could change.

Linda and I grabbed the suits and no sooner were we alone, we were both talking fast.

'Jesus!' exclaimed Linda in a loud whisper. 'Jesus! You just tore into that ass of a guy.'

'Shush, Linda! Don't use Jesus and ass in the same sentence, especially around here!' I responded, with a frown.

Linda laughed. 'What, you care?'

'I care plenty, but I'm not like those ill-mannered but well-meaning religious zealots who believe their faith gives them the right to be automatically correct about the status of everyone's soul, let alone that it's OK to be an insulting bully as long as it's in the name of Jesus.' By now I had worked up a bit of a lather, as my childhood Kentucky girlfriend Betty and her Mom used to say.

'So, are we doing this, or aren't we?' asked Linda. 'I'm sure that you've figured it out by now,' she added, cryptically.

'What do you mean?' I asked.

'What I mean is that this friendly, well meaning, but ill-mannered little diving outfit is a front, and Mr. Apollo, who's waiting out there for us, is most likely the ringleader,' she stated, matter-of-factly.

'So, are you saying that instead of throwing us to the lions, they're going to throw us to the sharks?' I remarked, as I started to remove my clothes.

'Ouch! Please don't say that,' winced Linda. 'But think about it for a minute. I still – and you can call me crazy –

want to do this, but I want you to wrap your head around it before we get in the boat.'

I paused to think. I was too upset to trust my gut, so I resorted to logic. 'No matter how extreme their beliefs are, murder, rape and bodily harm is a no-no in Jesus's eyes, let alone bad for business. Still, it would be prudent to ask where a phone is, so we can tell our local friends where we are and when we will be home for dinner.' My mind was also hatching getaway plots...

Linda started taking off her clothes with a sigh of relief and once again graced me with her big grin. 'I knew there was a reason I brought you along.'

We stood in front of each other in our wetsuits, each impressed. If we do say so, we looked pretty good, not *Sports Illustrated* good, but still enabling us to walk out of our little shack without dying of embarrassment.

'Are you ready to face the godling?' grinned Linda
'Hell, I'm not swimming with him, you are,' I shot back.
'Oh, yeah... I forgot,' she responded with a grin.

We set out in two boats after taking care of business and making our call. Greg, the godling, told us that the ocean floor extended about half a mile before slowly dropping. Where we were going was about 15 to 20 feet deep. After a few instructions and time checks, Greg took off with Linda, those two heading about a quarter mile further into deeper water. The young man with me was named Hal and was the quieter one of the two guys driving us to the beach, so that was somewhat reassuring.

Hal gave me a short lecture on how to use my flippers at the end of my feet.

'Now, since you've never done this before, you're going to wear a lifejacket the whole time,' he told me.

'I thought that lifejackets make you float,' said I as he strapped me in.

'They do, that's why I'm also putting this on you,' he replied, lifting up a belt with big squares attached to it.

'Here, feel,' he offered, handing me the belts. They weighed a ton. He snapped them on me. 'Don't worry,' he continued in a reassuring tone, 'in the water they won't feel half as heavy.'

'The jacket seems a little loose around the waist,' I

complained.

'No, you're ok. You don't want it too tight. Now, the weights will take you down like a stone to the bottom. You can then move around. If you have any kind of trouble just signal me. By pulling this cord you drop the weights and with very little effort you'll rise to the surface. Don't worry about the weights; I can find them easy. Just go to the surface if you need to for any reason.' He gave all our attachments one last check. He spat into his mask and told me to do the same, 'Helps keep the glass clear,' he explained. 'Ok, let's jump,' he said, looking me over with satisfaction.

The thought of being inside the aquarium looking out was very exciting. Yet, perched at the edge of the boat with my big flipper feet, it looked a long way down through the clear water to the bottom. Still I did not want to appear frightened or silly, so after only a second's hesitation I hopped out into the water and disappeared in one big gulp. The ocean had swallowed me whole, and the weights on the belt were pulling me, butt first, toward the ocean floor. It was as if I were descending down Alice's rabbit hole. Things were floating around me, flashing by before I could get a good look. In my mind was the image of

Dorothy in the tornado, things spinning all around her... Auntie Em! Auntie Em!

Oh Gods, I thought, *too much oxygen already. I'd better get a grip!* The next thing I knew I was deposited, quite unceremoniously, on my behind on the ocean floor. The life jacket was hunched around my ears like two big orange rabbit ear pillows, so I could only see right in front of me. A very attractive blue fish with big curious eyes was checking me out closely, no doubt optimistic that I would soon be a source of food. With my rear firmly nailed to the ocean floor and the big orange life jacket sticking up like ungainly ears or wings I must have looked like a huge bug flailing about on its back.

I caught a glimpse of Hal and signaled him to come over. He pulled me to my feet, and I pointed to the life jacket. He pulled it down and I held it while he found the straps. I was trying hard not to give him the 'I told you so' look as he held me down, with one big foot over both my little feet to hold me steady as he re-strapped me in. I was finally secure, like a Victorian lady in her corset. He then helped me walk and swim in a more traditional manner.

Now this is more like it, I thought.

Hal asked me whether I was all right. I nodded. He steadied me in an upright position, showing me how to gently paddle my feet and keep myself that way and then indicated that he was going to swim around a bit nearby.

Fine, I thought, as he gracefully swam away through the water. *You do that while I take this all in.*

It's really true what they say, I thought. *Snorkeling gives you a taste of what it's like but it's not until you dive that you can fully appreciate that you truly are in a different and alien world from our own... you're not in Kansas anymore.*

I slowly turned in place and took in the sights. I was in a little meadow of sand, so to speak. There were various little rocks and reefs. In the distance I could see larger fish, but it was hard to see exactly how big. The fish close to me darted about and appeared as pretty little jewels of the sea. By the time I turned fully around I could not see Hal anywhere, not even his bubbles. I had a general idea of the direction he had gone, yet he was nowhere to be seen. My breathing had calmed down, so I took a step forward.

Whoa ahhh! I was upside down. *How in the hell did that happen?* I twisted around but kept spinning, much to my dismay. I was twirling around in the water like some sort of maimed octopus. More of the silly blue fish showed up. Looking back on it, years later, I realized they looked just like Dory in the movie *Saving Nemo*. They were very curious and annoying at the time. They kept looking at me as if thinking: *are you trying to be entertaining or you are just dying?* I finally managed to get my butt back down, my legs in front, and my head somewhat up. I would try to turn slowly, either to get my feet under me or at least be on my belly, so I could swim a little. I managed to look about some more and again was so awed at what a different alien world I was in, like a huge fishbowl. I looked closely at rocks and bits of plantlike creatures clinging to what they could. However, before too long it became apparent to me that, because of the way the weights were placed on my body, the only way I could easily stand more erect was if someone were holding my hand. I floated a few feet above the ocean floor and tried to wiggle my way toward something that was tall enough for me to grab onto and pull myself up. No such luck... I could see no way for me to get around under those circumstances and the effort of dealing with it all was using up oxygen. Hal, moreover, was nowhere to be found.

I centered myself again and looked about. It was beautiful and yet, because here the rocks were low in the sand, there weren't many places to hide, except in one direction. This was most likely where Hal was, unless he was watching me from above somewhere. I had not looked. I suddenly felt very alone. I looked in every direction for Hal, or for his bubbles, but there was nothing, so it certainly seemed like I was all alone. Even though I was feeling a little more in control, I still realized that to truly enjoy the experience, I needed help or at least a guide. It was all so new, magical, and a little scary, and it occurred to me I should have insisted that Linda and I stick together, even if I had stayed by the boat. I looked around one more time for Hal, when I saw that I was drifting toward dark shadows by some rocks and coral. Now, I just wanted to be back on the beach. I had no idea where Linda was, and I realized that I was not sharing this experience with her. My gut was telling me that we had been separated for a reason other than just the fact she was experienced at diving. I realized also that we were being lied to in more than one way. These people were behaving more along the lines of some sort of Christian order or cult, and we were being toyed with. I didn't want to play anymore. It also occurred to me that Hal might not be far off and maybe he could see me, but I didn't care now if he could see me or not. It was not that my feelings were hurt, rather I was just plain pissed. I felt betrayed as a person, and as a customer who had paid money for a safe and enjoyable dive.

Oddly enough, even with me being a bit of a student of history and religion, and aware of how unpleasant the results of clashes of belief and culture can be, my Christian upbringing of faith kicked in and I also remembered that we were Pele's guest. This allowed me to feel I could trust this situation, not panic, but just think things through. Hal leaving me drifting willy-nilly all alone out here during my first scuba dive was dangerous and not very nice. I started to feel like what the fish thought I looked like – an out of place, dying bug. I pulled myself together and took hold of the situation. Taking a last look around at the wonder of the world of the sea, I pulled my cord. The weights dropped off, and I immediately started to rise gracefully (praise the gods) to the surface.

My head popped up through the water, and I was bobbing like a cork. The sky had clouded over slightly in the twenty to thirty minutes or, so we'd been down. I bobbed over to the boat. Hal was not there, and I realized that this was one of those deals where one had to throw one's leg over the side and pull yourself over into the boat. However, I was not having any more humiliation on any terms but my own. I looked at the shore. It was quite a distance away – a half mile, maybe more. I figured out my angle of approach and started paddling.

I'd not gone too far when I heard 'Hey! Hey!' over the water.

I chose to ignore it and kept dog paddling. Next, I heard an engine starting up and soon Hal was puttering by me in the boat.

'Hey! What are you doing?' he asked, 'Why did you come up so early? I could see you most of the time, you know. I can try and give you a hand into the boat...'

'Sooo... now we're being helpful...' I responded in a sarcastic tone. I kept moving.

'Awww... Don't be mad. If you can't get into the boat, I'll tow you in,' he offered hopefully.

'Look, I'm not going to be towed into shore on a line like some half-dead porpoise. I'll swim in as far as I can and when I have some footing I'll walk in,' I stated firmly.

'But you're not even swimming,' he wailed, 'you're dog paddling!'

'Damn straight I am! I can't do much else in this life jacket anyway. So, I'm making a beeline toward the shore. Here…' I unclipped my scuba gear. 'Take this. I can swim better without it. You can watch me or go back to Greg's boat, which I think I see way out there, and high tail it back before I drown or make it to shore.' With that, I turned away and headed toward shore.

Not looking very happy, Hal turned toward Greg's boat and puttered off. I resumed valiantly dogpaddling to shore. The flippers were making it a lot easier and fortunately the light waves were pushing me toward shore, but still, after about ten minutes, I could feel the strain of the position in which the lifejacket was holding my body. I could also see that I was indeed closer to shore. I turned around and saw Hal by Greg's boat. It looked like he and Linda were back from their underwater excursion.

This renewed my determination to get to the beach under my own steam. It also caused me to make a somewhat risky decision. The life jacket was thankfully a lot easier to get off than on. Having the jacket off was a relief, but now I had to figure out a way to tow it somehow and swim. A little creative thinking gave me an idea. I put the jacket sideways around my waist and lay on it so that it held me up a little but did not interfere with me doing a kind of side stroke. The flippers now moved me right along at a steady comfortable pace.

I could already see the bottom of the ocean and knew the water was not as deep as before. I looked up and watched how the gentle waves were moving in toward the beach. It occurred to me that there might be rocks and reefs that I could hurt myself on, so if I saw a wave bubbling up or breaking, I moved away. Soon, I could see I was over the lava rock shelf that jutted out toward the ocean and not long after that I knew I could stand on it. However, the safer and faster thing was to keep swimming for as long as I could.

Soon, though, I had no choice but to stand, and I was stalking through the water like a stork in Bozo shoes because I kept the flippers on for safety. I took them off only when I could see clearly where I was stepping. Soon there was a good layer of soft sand.

When I reached the shore, I dropped the life jacket to the sand and caught my breath. It did not take long after that for me to hear the puttering of the boat engines. Linda jumped out, looking a little pale. She walked by me heading toward the changing shack

'You were right,' she said as she walked by me.

'Right? Right about what?' I asked as I caught up with her.

'Lions and sharks,' was all she said in reply.

Once in the changing shack, Linda told me of her adventures as we wiggled out of our wet suits. I initiated her tale by asking, 'So, what do you mean, lions and sharks?'

'Not too hard to figure it out, dear,' she said with a sigh.

'No!' I exclaimed. 'Not on purpose!'

'Oh yes, very much on purpose. Granted it was a giant

old nurse shark but damn that mother was big!'

'Oh my God! Tell me the whole story from the beginning,' I demanded.

'Well, it's like I suspected; Greg's the big cheese and took over from some guy who retired. They all consider themselves disciples of sorts, fishing souls for Jesus. It's all part of the business plan. I ended up with Greg because of my family background. In their eyes I'm just about a lost cause, a real hard case. You, on the other hand, you are still "rescuable" because, from their perspective, I'm just plain lost because I'm born out of two related but still non-Christian religions. Somehow, they consider you just confused, so naturally you've lost your way.'

'How kind of them to share this wisdom with you,' I added dryly.

'So,' continued Linda, 'by the time we were ready to dive we had got the whole "can I introduce you to Jesus" discussion out of the way. Then after a few instructions about what we were going to do, Greg asked me if I'd like to see some caves. I said, sure, as long as he went in first. So, we tooled around for a few minutes. The water was clear, and we looked at some cool stuff first, but then he took me to this cave. He told me to wait and he went in first. Coming back out, Greg gave me the all clear. I went in and there on the bottom of this cave was this huge shark.'

'How big?' I asked.

'Oh, it felt like twenty feet but most likely it was between ten to twelve. It was a good-sized female nurse shark. It was because I'm so afraid of them I took the time as a kid to learn all I could about them. So, I knew I was pretty safe in there because nurse sharks very seldom attack people but...' Linda shuddered a bit while pulling on her clothes.

'Did you say anything to him?' I asked

'Nope,' she answered. 'Partly because I was so shocked

and angry and partly because I did not want to give him the satisfaction.'

'I want you to trust me on this, Linda, because I'm going to say something to these guys,' I said with a steely glint in my eyes.

By all means; be my guest.' She grinned.

I waited until we were back at the office and Greg was by his desk. I walked up to him and said directly and flatly, 'We want our money back.'

Greg rolled his eyes. 'What possible reason could you have to justify me doing that?'

'That's easy,' I answered. 'Because I'll list for you all the same ones I'll give to your local and Honolulu business bureau, so you'll have a good heads up if this little chat of ours does not go so well.'

'I gave you a safe dive. It's not my fault if you took off early and came to shore,' Greg replied with a controlled snotty tone.

'Ah, a safe dive. Let's address that first.' I then mused. 'On one hand, yes, you and Hal took some precautions physically showing us basic things. I, though, have some issues with safety regarding myself. Hal says he knew I was safe, but I certainly did not know that because he was nowhere to be found! Still, besides that little fact, how about emotionally safe, mentally safe and spiritually safe? Not by a long shot.'

Greg sat down in his chair behind his desk. 'I don't understand what you mean,' he said.

'Oh yes, you do,' I shot back. 'You're a smart guy and a businessperson but on the chance you don't, I will enlighten you. Number one, there is this little thing called honesty and ethical practices in business that caters to the public.'

'Whatever I say here is protected by freedom of speech laws,' he interjected, crossing his long arms and glowering up at me from his chair.

'Great! Then you have the freedom to put in all your advertisements that you are a Christian business and run your business accordingly. All are welcome, but if you're not comfortable being witnessed to and discussing religious matters, this may not be the diving outfit for you. Truthful and honest; values that are high on Jesus's list of concepts to live by, as I recall.

Number two,' I continued; 'Basic business ethics. You can't be a religious organization masquerading as a diving school. You are either a diving school that happens to be run by Christians. Or you are a religious organization that happens to provide diving services. You see what I mean?

Number three – leaving a person with no diving experience alone, or even letting them think they are alone, is irresponsible and cruel. Shame on you.

Number four, the whole shark thing really takes the cake.'

'Hey!' protested Greg, pointing at Linda. 'She's actually a good diver. I was just trying to help her get over her fear of sharks!' Mr. Body Beautiful now morphed into a seventh-grade boy, slouching back in his chair, pouting with irritation.

'So, you're practicing psychiatry here as well?' I retorted. 'I think you'd better decide just what you *are* doing here and be sure you have a license for it. Now, where's our money?'

Back downtown, by the hotel, Linda was counting the money while I looked up at the sky. It was still cloudy with partial sun, and the wind was picking up a bit. I was also amazed that after all we had been through it was only just after mid-afternoon. Time seemed to run at a different pace in Hawaii. I mentioned this to Linda.

'Hey! Then we still have time to do it!' exclaimed Linda happily.

'Time to do what?' I asked, somewhat surprised. I was

tired and grumpy. I just wanted to find a quiet spot to lie down for a while.

'My helicopter ride!'

'You've got to be kidding me,' I replied.

The heliport was not that far away. My mood had not improved any, but Linda promised me up and down that if I sniffed anything amiss, we were out of there. We went up to the ticket desk where several people were working.

'Hello.' I managed to be cordial. 'I have a few questions.'

I soon found out that there was one possible flight left, the last one of the day. They were just waiting for the weather report before they could get permission to take off.

'If this flight is able to take off, miss, would you like to reserve it?' asked the nice woman behind the desk.

'Yes, I would, but I have another question.' I waited until she looked up so that I had her full attention. 'Is this organization a front for a church or any religious organization?

'Excuse me?' She furrowed her brow.

'What I mean to ask is, when we are in the air will anyone ask us about Jesus and whether or not our souls are saved?' I clarified.

Two other people joined the woman behind the desk. They looked at me with big eyes I had the feeling, or perhaps just feared, that somewhere a finger was poised over a panic button.

'We have lots of churches here that do that witness and such, but all we do here is give helicopter rides,' one of them responded.

'Well, I'm certainly glad to hear it, because we had one hell of a morning,' I said.

At this point Linda cleared her throat and broke in and explained our story.

'Wow, I go to church every Sunday, but I would never do that to any *haoli*,' said a very Hawaiian-looking woman.

'And the part about the shark! You were way too nice to them. I'd have called the sheriff. So, what can we do, dear, to make this trip happy for you besides offer you some punch or coffee?'

'Well,' I said, 'everywhere we've been we've tried to honor the Hawaiian gods. And I'd like to do that here if you have a good spot for it.'

'Anyone in particular?' asked the nice lady.

'Pele and Lono come to mind.'

'The volcano!' said everyone behind the desk at once.

'But I have no offerings and...'

'Here's an apple,' said the Hawaiian woman, opening her big purse very merrily. 'Works fine in a pinch. In front of the building are all kinds of flowers. You can help yourself to make a *lei*.'

'That's so kind of you. On the other island we had a proper *lei*.'

'This is a water volcano, dear,' she broke in. 'And you are honoring Lono as well, so flowers will be fine and so will the apple.'

This reassured me, and she waved us out the door.

Linda spotted the helicopter pilot and went over to speak to him while I started picking flowers, ignoring the tourists that were giving me strange looks for what must have seemed like very odd behavior. I allowed myself a thirty-second fantasy whereby I put the flowers in my hair and did a little dance while singing 'Hare Hare Krishna', which was still somewhat popular at that time, especially around airports. It was a fun thought, and coupled with the desk people's kindness, it put me back in a good mood.

At that point, Linda came running up with a guy who looked like a pilot who had seen interesting days.

'We gotta go, we gotta go now! If we're going to pull this off,' he announced. 'Grab your purse and the flowers and let's go! We've only got a window of four knots.'

'What does that mean?' I asked Linda as she stuffed me

into the back of the copter.

'It means that if the wind blows only four knots faster, we won't be able to do it because we'll be over the wind safety limit.'

'Oh boy!'

From the minute we took off we could feel the wind buffeting the copter.

'Ooooooweee!' cried the pilot out cheerily, 'This could blow us all the way to Maui!'

Oh, great, I thought. *We have Indiana Jones for a helicopter pilot.*

'I think the best thing to do is take a quick spin over some of the sights and that will give me time to see if the winds hold steady enough, and that we have the power to actually to get over the volcano safely. Four knots don't give you much of a fudge factor.' The pilot grinned broadly.

It was really quite impossible to say beautiful as many times as it deserved to be said as we zipped over waterfalls, lush valleys and breathtaking shorelines. It flashed by all too fast, it seemed, for us to take it all in.

Our state of awe was broken by our pilot announcing combat style, 'I'm going in!' The way he said it made me think that perhaps he'd served in Vietnam – which I hoped was the case, as it made me feel safer.

Then suddenly we knew what he meant. The whole helicopter started shaking as it struggled against the wind. Every part of the chopper vibrated, it felt like some giant had lassoed the helicopter's tail and was holding us still in the sky. We hovered like a hummingbird as we tried to get over a mountainous green ridge.

'Not everyone gets to see or do this, you know,' the pilot shouted over the noise. 'It's always a crap shoot if Lono lets you come over the mountain and if Pele will let you see her, especially on days like this. Here!' He tossed Linda a small bottle, while he shouted over the blades and wind. 'That's to go with the flowers but you got to pour it out. She likes it and we could use a little help.'

I looked at what Linda had in her hand and it was a small airplane bottle of gin.

The helicopter started shaking harder than ever. My first time in a chopper was becoming quite frightening. I closed my eyes and told both Pele and Lono that I had been brave under water and now I was having to be brave in the air as well; a little mercy would really be appreciated here. There was a strange popping sound and it felt as if we were released from our bonds, like a rubber band snap, and with a scream of 'Yeeeeehaaa!' from our pilot we were over the ridge.

'Well I'll be …' he continued, and the next words we heard from him were: 'Get ready to do your thing, girls, because the gods are being really nice to you. Pele must like you. Take a look out and down the left window.'

We looked out of the window. We were flying over an amazing water-filled crater surrounded by dark emerald vegetation. To our even greater amazement, a perfect rainbow sat in a great circle around the entire mouth of the crater. The giant circle glinted with diamond sparkling water spray. It was breathtaking. The pilot brought us lower. I opened the window and Linda opened the little bottle and poured. I threw in the flowers, kissed the apple and tossed that to Pele as well. We watched it all disappear into the crater.

'What a rare sight! I think you guys made it all worth it because frankly this was a bit crazy even for me!' shouted the pilot over his shoulder with a big grin.

By the time we got back to our hosts we had *such* tales to tell. Robert promised to inquire discreetly about the diving company. He told us that he believed in spreading the good news, but ambush Christianity was smacking a bit too much like religious fascism to him. Also, when saying grace at dinner, he thanked Jesus that we had been kept safe during our adventures.

We slept like rocks that night. The next day we reported in to Victor before leaving the house.

'This is better than I had hoped for,' he said. 'All the signs are good. You now have one more island and two more official tasks before you. Call me when you arrive there.'

Linda started pulling out her swimsuit. 'What are you doing?' I asked.

'You heard him. All the signs are good, which means more unknowns ahead, so we have half a day to relax before our next plane hop back to the Big island. Sara told me about a peaceful beach, and there's a cute little girl who wants to come with along with us.' Linda pointed to the door to Lori as she poked her head around the corner with a shy smile.

We grabbed some towels, headed for the door and on the way out I paused by Lono's cross on the wall, smiled, and whispered, *Mahalo Lono*.

Part VIII

The Power of Innocence

The Hawaiian Islands lie like rainbowed jewels in the shimmering, everchanging sea. Some call them 'The Footprints of Pele'. There, she made her stand and walked in the domain of Great Mother, Uli. With her own fire, Pele formed the land she would call her own. Linda and I were more aware than ever that we were walking on the lands and paths that others not only call home, but know as sacred, and to keep our eyes and ears open and not assume anything. We rented a car and drove to a small town to call upon Mike, the brother of a dear friend of mine. He invited us to stay at his home. It was such a treat to meet his lovely wife and children. I learned how to make coconut pudding. Then they took us to some lovely beaches.

The next day Mike advised us to drive up to a place called Queen's Baths to swim – he told us we would not regret it – and then stop by the visitor center further up the highway because it was worthwhile to do so.

Queen's Baths turned out to be a lovely little grotto surrounded by shady and twisty trees. Linda got out of the car, hands on hips, surveying the scene.

'This is really a peaceful and beautiful place,' she said. 'I'm going to go back to that little store I saw and get us some food. We can picnic after we swim. Sound like a plan?'

'Sounds like a plan to me. Meet you in the pond.' I grabbed my towel and bathing suit.

As Linda drove off, a large van pulled up. The side door slid open and out spilled over half a dozen children aged between about 5 to 10 and from as many cultures. A young woman with long, blond mini braids popped her head out of the car and shouted, 'I'll be back in an hour and a half! Remember the rules!'

'Yes, Katie!' shouted back the little chorus of munchkins as they rushed past me to the water, carrying towels, pails, toys and little fishing nets.

A little girl in pigtails stopped in front of me. 'You're new here, aren't you?' she asked.

'Yes, this is my first time,' I replied.

'I thought so,' she said, taking charge by grabbing my hand and taking me to the edge of the pond. 'If you've never been here before, the pond kinda looks like a big black hole until the sun is right overhead. I'll show you the best place to step in,' she said, very reassuringly. 'But first of all, you need to go to changing rock,' she continued, while pointing to a large boulder with bushes around it.

Inside was a well-used little hollow where countless people must have changed their clothes.

'Thank you very much. You're very kind. What's your name?' I asked, while I pulled my suit on with the little girl standing guard.

'June. I was named after the month I was borned in.'

'Oh, I see, my name is Cor-nae-lee-a. That's kinda long.'

June giggled. 'It's a little long, but my Hawaiian middle name is much bigger,' she announced proudly.

We stepped back out to the water.

'Now, pay attention,' the little girl instructed. 'This is where you step to get in the pond slow, unless you want to jump in like the boys.'

The boys were happily taking wild leaps or cannonballs into the water.

'I'm really surprised that you kids got left all alone here,' I said, as we daintily put our toes in the water and gently slipped into the cool dark pond. 'I have to ask. Don't you have a "don't speak to strangers" rule?'

June rolled her little eyes. 'This is Hawaii. Everybody speaks to strangers. Besides, we look out for each other, like right now you're the grown-up in the pond and by the time you leave someone else will come along.'

'I see...' I said as I started paddling about. 'By the way, I'm curious. What are the rules Katie was talking about?

'Number 1,' started June in a sing-song voice. 'Always stay together unless someone's family comes for them. Number 2, if no grown-up is around and someone is hurt, run to the store for help. Number 3, when you're playing and horsing around, don't do anything stupid. That one is a real hard one for the boys to keep,' she added, dropping her sweet voice to a whisper.

'Is that it?' I asked

'That's it,' she replied, diving under the water like a little mermaid. She popped up again in the middle of the pond.

'Come on!' She waved me over. 'Let's see how many guppies David has caught!'

I started to swim her way, rolling over on my back to look up. The sun was sparkling through the trees. There were plants and orchid flowers growing out of the cliff rocks, which curved around and above a good part of the pond. I swam up to the rest of the children who were crowded at the edge of the pond with one boy carefully holding a glass jar and another with a little green toy bucket.

'Yeah!' He shouted out in triumph, looking in the bucket. 'I got the big one again with the long tail. Time for you to come visit me again, fishy,' said the boy who must be David. He looked to be about 5 or 6.

I swam up to him. 'Can I see?' I asked.

'Sure, this is Freddy, he's my favorite fish. I catch him, take him home for a week or so, and when I think he's getting homesick I bring him back.' David beamed with pride.

I held up the jar to see a male guppy with a long rainbow tail

'There must be a million Freddies in this pond,' said another boy, older by two or three years.

'Oh, shut up Hilo!' shot back June with startling authority 'If David says it's Freddy, it's Freddy.'

Freddy was carefully transferred from the bucket to the glass jar.

'Hey, what's everyone looking at?' asked Linda walking up back from the store.

'This is my friend Linda,' I announced. 'And we are looking at the guppies that David here has caught.'

'You mean minnows,' corrected Linda.

'No, guppies. May I?' I asked the boy with the jar, which I handed up to Linda to examine.

'Well, how about that! They are guppies!' chuckled Linda. 'Do you think there are any guppies big enough in that pond worth catching and frying up for lunch.' She asked teasingly while eyeing Freddy in the jar.

'Eeeeewwwww!' exclaimed the children in a chorus all around me.

David practically levitated out of the pond and reclaimed his fishy from Linda. 'Guppies are not for eating,' he stated with a furrowed brow.

'Oh, David she was only teasing. Everyone knows that, except Hilo who catches them with his mouth,' said June, with a wrinkled nose.

'Hey! I spit them back out! And they're just fine,' Hilo defended himself.

Linda and I looked at Hilo and together we gave him a big EEEEeeeeeeUUUUU! like the children had done. Everyone laughed.

June then climbed out the water, doing her apparent duties by showing Linda the changing rock and standing guard for her as well. We then proceeded to have a good time chasing the kids by pretending to be alligators because sharks didn't seem to faze these kids as much. Plus, Linda said she'd as soon pretend to be a platypus than a shark, so alligators it was. The kids were squealing and splashing all around, so everyone, especially us, got a good workout. It seemed like all too soon that Katie was back for her charges. She was happy to hear that David actually wanted to nap as he crawled into the van, still clutching Freddy in his jar. A chorus of *aloha*s sounded, and the grotto was quiet and peaceful once more as we ate our lunch. Looking back at that moment in time, I realize how precious it all was. What a gift such a place is, and what a gift to each other we and the children were to share such innocent joy.

After our lunch, we found and took the route to the large visitor center we'd been told about. There should also be a phone through which we could check in with Victor. The huge visitor center we came upon had large signs telling of Hawaii's past, including the practice of human sacrifice. The place turned out to be joined to a museum with an information center. Such a cross between tourist center and a proper museum felt a little bit odd, particularly with regards to the subject matter. We found a phone there and called Victor. I told him about this center and asked him if the Hawaiians thought about sacrifice in the same way that other cultures do, including those of the Middle East, Africa and Mexico.

'That is a very complex subject, no matter what culture one considers,' Victor replied. 'Hawaii was introduced to human sacrifice by a priest who came there from far Tahitian islands and changed Hawaii's way of life. It was in the time that sacrifice spread like a cancer around our planet, becoming much more common place. Like I said, it is a complex subject. Many people today don't realize that any kind of human war and terrorism, ancient or modern, is also a sacrifice. Blood that is spilled upon the earth in battle with courage and in honest heart, especially for a noble cause, can be understandable and even righteous. Yet, if most people were really truthful with themselves and looked deep into their hearts, they would know that the gods who love this earth are saddened by our human violence, and the countless unnecessary deaths committed through evil, greed, ignorance, ego or pure foolishness.'

'What you've said rings deeply true in my heart,' I replied over the phone. 'Yet, I must ask, Victor, why are we here in this place, on this earth and in this moment? I mean I think I know what my intentions are by my being your voice here, which of course is an important honor, and I know what we are praying about. But is there something else that's driving this journey?'

'It is many things,' Victor answered warmly. 'In every moment and in every place, you go, you are being given knowledge, the opportunity to learn and the tools to play your part. Where you need to go now is to a birthplace. It is there where history changed, not only for Hawaii but for the world as well. You must go north and there along the coast you will come across two *heiaus*, one is very large, the other is small and a little harder to find, but both are very important for very different reasons. It is there that you must go and make an offering. You will then know the last thing you must do before you leave Hawaii.'

'You said those sites constitute a birthplace. What do you mean, exactly?' I asked.

'It is the birthplace of a king,' he answered solemnly. 'You will find it and you will know what to do once you get there. Pay attention and don't overthink things. Be logical yet open, as it is your greatest talent.' Victor murmured a blessing and hung up before I could say anything else.

Heading North was no problem because we were going to stop by where my friend's brother Mike worked. We had spent some time with him and his lovely family. Now we were meeting him at his old workplace, which turned out to be a beautiful hotel with a lovely cove and beach right behind it.

'This place has quite the story,' Mike stated as he met us in front of the hotel and began conducting his personal tour. 'I've been living in Hawaii for over fifteen years and was here working my first job when they started building this hotel. The locals were quite upset because this was considered sacred land and an important part of Hawaii's history. From the very beginning the project was plagued with accidents and things going wrong. The workers begged their bosses to bring in a *kahuna*, but they said that, in such a big project, things happen and with all the lovely additions they were going to do to honor Hawaii's history the spirits should be appeased.'

Mike paused dramatically and we all took a deep breath as he continued his story, now describing the grand opening with important people from even the mainland attending.

'I believe it was a congressman and his wife who awakened in the middle of the night to the sounds of chanting. Thinking it was something that the local people would be doing, they both went back to sleep. The congressman was reawakened not long after to the sound of his wife screaming. Her face contorted in terror, she pointed to a glowing man in a red feather cape and curved headdress, standing at the foot of the bed. Then, to their further horror, the red-caped Hawaiian man disappeared right in front of their eyes. Terrified, the congressional couple ran out of the bedroom in their nightclothes. The terrified staff, together with security, had to retrieve their things and take them to another hotel. A *kahuna* was called immediately and came the next day. He undertook three days of ceremonies to appeal to and appease the anger of the spirits and the powerful ghost of this place. Then he performed a blessing and extended an offering to the animal guardian of this part of the waters. That offering partially consisted of a large bundle of meat and greens that was tied to a line and thrown out into the cove. "You watch this good!" the *kahuna* told me. "Don't let anyone touch it until the offering has been taken."

"Oh, that's not going to take very long," I responded, pointing to the bopping bundle. Fish, small sharks, and little rays were already nibbling at it.

'The *kahuna* smiled, 'There is a lot of food there, he said. "Believe me, they will get out of the way when the one who it is meant for comes."

'The *kahuna* left, and I tended to my duties nearby for about an hour. On my returning to the bundle to check on its status, the sun was setting. I was tired and wondering if that old *kahuna* was expecting me to stay up all night watching the damn thing. At that point, I saw a huge shadow in the water. The hair on the back of my neck started to stand on end. There was not another fish of any kind to be seen in the aqua cove. In water that was only a few feet deep, yet just enough to accommodate its great size, was the biggest Manta Ray I have ever seen in my life approaching the bundle. As quietly and respectfully as I could, I walked up the little pier sticking out into the water and untied the rope holding the bundle. This was a king, a grandfather of all mantas, and its wings must have been at least sixteen or more feet across. As soon as the bundle was free, the King Manta grabbed it and took off toward the open water and the setting sun. It was a moment I will never forget,' Mike finished.

Linda and I were standing there, completely awed. 'Well,' said Linda, breaking the silence, 'that was quite a story and speaking of bundles, I could certainly eat one myself.'

Mike laughed. 'This very hotel is quite famous for their *luaus*, but they cost quite a bundle.' He smiled. 'You might be better off eating at some of the local fare in town. I know a place that serves very good *poi*.'

He gave us instructions where to go and, before taking his leave, informed us that *poi* is a truly wondrous thing, as it comes in one of several shades, from white to purple, and in several consistencies and flavors. It resembles something like pudding and perhaps Malt-O-Meal and lands on one's plate with a big flop. People either love it or hate it, but it is a regular staple on any Hawaiian table, together with Spam. *Poi* is made from the *taro* root and many a Hawaiian would have starved to death on long ocean voyages if not for the *taro* root. It is very versatile, sometimes sour, which goes well with meat, or sometimes sweeter, which goes well with eggs. This café was most certainly a local one because *poi* came with everything here, along with the Spam. Eggs and Spam with *poi*. Pancakes with Spam and *poi*. Fruit and *poi*. Steak, eggs and *poi*.

'Now, that last one sounds like a winner,' Linda observed. So, steak, eggs and *poi* it was. The *poi* served to us was a deep lavender purple color and tasted like a slightly sour pudding. It actually complimented the meat quite well. We left there feeling fortified and ready for anything.

Now heading north up the coast, we saw the terrain change from sandy shores to black fields of lava spilling out to the sea. There were signs pointing the way to ancient petroglyphs, caves and fishing sites of long ago, which we decided to pass on and continued northward. Sticking close to the shore, we came to a part of the road where it turned sharply inland toward the right, with a big sign showing the way to the Birthplace of King Kamehameha. This must be the birthplace that Victor had spoken of. Another turn to the left led up to what was a small National Guard station, which was closer to the shore

'We're going into a National Guard Station, aren't we?' asked Linda with a raised brow.

'Yep, looks like the only way to go, since Victor said to stay close to the coast.' And with that I turned on in.

The place seemed deserted, like everyone had gone fishing deserted. We drove slowly past a collection of buildings with a small playground in the front yard. Any moment, we thought, someone would step out, but no one did so. We continued to drive through the facility until we came to a closed cattle gate over the road.

'We are going through that gate somehow, I take it,' said Linda.

'Looks that way,' I replied.

'A gate usually indicates private property, you know,' mused Linda.

'True, true, but there are no signs saying, "do not enter" and no one is stopping us,' I offered.

'It's still a closed gate,' she grinned in reply.

'Well, let's see what we can do about that,' I said as I opened the car door. 'If it's meant to be, we should have no problem.' With this, I walked to the gate, which had a flip over latch but no lock. I opened the gate.

Linda slid over and drove on through while I shut the gate behind the car.

We continued to drive, still on a bumpy dirt road, with

the ocean to our left, its deep aqua waves crashing onto a rocky shore. Soon we were outside a long and square stone wall on our right side. There was something about it. On stopping the car, I emerged, standing on the car door entrance to get a better look. There was another, smaller wall inside the larger one, with a further small wall inside that one, all of which reminded me a little of a labyrinth, with its pieces affording a mazelike effect. I could not see this labyrinth's center very well from the car, but the whole structure appeared very old and was made of stone unlike the lava rock making up the other *heiaus* we had seen. There was also a vibe around the place that was tangible.

'This must be the older *heiau* that Victor mentioned and that places the larger one up the road, meaning we are in the right place,' I remarked.

We drove about an eighth of a mile further and there it was, rising from a hill overlooking the ocean with its big black lava walls pointing up toward the sky. The road we were on curved around as we proceeded up towards it. We then found ourselves in a parking area in front of a big sign explaining the site. This *heiau* had quite a history, including being a place for human sacrifice at one time. It was also a site that was still being used and was watched over by a female *kahuna*. Again, looking around us, we appeared to be alone except for one empty car nearby. The day had been warm with bright sun, but here on this windy hill, with the sun making its way to the horizon, there was a slight nip to the air. A voice floated on the breeze.

'Hey, did you hear that?' I asked Linda.

'Yeah, sounds like chanting coming from in there,' Linda answered, nodding toward the entranceway of the high black walled *heiau*. We were taking a few steps towards it when a group of women appeared, walking out of the structure. There were five of them, and as soon as they saw us four of the women moved to stand protectively around the fifth; a taller , imposing Hawaiian woman dressed very traditionally with flowers in her hair. Linda tilted her hat toward me.

'Well, this is your department,' she stated. 'I'm going to head down to the ocean and commune with nature. You do your thing, and good luck.'

With that, Linda turned on her heel to stride down the road, leaving me to face what we both knew must be the *kahuna* of this place. I turned my attention back toward the five Hawaiian ladies and, to my surprise, all five approached me cautiously. Four of them wore lovely, colorful, and perfectly wrapped sarong-type dresses, while the *kahuna* wore a traditional *muu muu* dress. None of them had a hair out of place, and all five walked with grace and dignity, with the wind barely moving their clothes. As they approached, I was painfully aware of the fact that here I was, wearing only my faithful wooden sandals and a long cotton jersey dress. To make matters worse, the wind made a little dirt devil that danced around me. My waist length hair was blown about in all directions as if I'd stuck my finger in a light socket. I felt that I was quite the sight. I kept my hands deep in my pockets, making sure that my dress stayed at a respectable level. To these women, I was sure, I must have looked like some windblown wild child. They stopped about eight feet in front of me and the wind dropped to a gentle breeze.

I managed a smile as I realized that, in my haste that morning, I had placed in my pockets Victor's slip of paper and one of my crystals. I pulled my hands out of my pockets as I said a cheery but slightly nervous *aloha*. Four of the approaching women, on seeing my hands come out of my pockets, started to move closer to their *kahuna*.

The *kahuna* waved them away with a small indication of one hand. '*Aloha*,' she responded in a kindly tone.

I realized that she knew and understood that my hands had been hidden deep in my pockets to keep my dress down. By the look on the *kahuna*'s face, she seemed amused, and I was both embarrassed and amused by my frazzled state. At that moment all I could focus on was what to say that wouldn't make me sound like some sort of New Age hippie nut case. The wind blew again and there was a bellowing sigh audible within it. This caught the attention of all of us, making us look up and focus out on the ocean. The women followed my gaze. There, out in the sea, was a large pod of blue whales. Their massive bodies were jumping and singing, their trumpeting sounds blowing in the wind.

The *kahuna* turned to me, surprised. 'This is not the time of year when the whales sing and dance here. They are here because of you. Who are you?' she demanded, in a firm and even tone.

I handed her the slip of paper containing Victor's name and introduced myself. Following this, I also handed the *kahuna* the crystal I had in my pocket and told her stones such as this were part of the offerings I'd been making to the gods. She looked at it closely, looked again at the piece of paper, then handed them both back to me.

'The name is quite a claim,' she observed.

'So, I've been told, but nothing Victor claims surprises me anymore. The crystals have been part of my offerings with fruit and proper *leis*. I know it's not all traditional here, but somehow it felt right, and it seems so far the gods are OK with it.'

'I see. So, why are you here? I will take you on as a student if that is what you and he wish,' the *kahuna* stated in a matter of a fact way.

'My eyes widened. 'Oh my!' I replied. 'I'm much honored and would certainly do so if I could stay in Hawaii, but I must go back home to California after this trip.'

'You will come back,' the *kahuna* said, 'sooner than you think, but it will be a long time before we meet again. Bring that unusual crystal with you and I will remember. Is it cut that way, or does it grow that way in the earth?

'That is the way it grows,' I answered. 'To me, it is very symbolic of all the natural magic right in the earth.'

'And so, it is.' She smiled. 'Yet, that is not why you are here. Which gods have you been giving offerings to?'

'To Pele, Uli and Lono,' I replied.

'This *heiau* is dedicated to Ku and I am the *kahuna* here.'

'Yes, I read the sign. He is the god of warriors and war.'

'Yes.' She nodded. 'Very much like the Christian god, Jehovah.'

'Is it possible maybe that this could be part of the human problem?' I offered. 'That we're giving so much of our faith, energy and worship to a god. Even if you see them all as one, the part that is getting all the attention is a god of war. Ultimately it can only mean human sacrifice, no matter how it is dressed up or disguised.'

'You speak of very deep and dark mysteries where it is said that even angels fear to tread,' the *kahuna* replied, a little sadly. 'Ku has many ways. Yet, this is the path that humans have chosen to take. Yes, one priest introduced Ku with the ways of war and sacrifice. Still, the people chose this way again, as it appealed to the chiefs and because they were afraid. Also, it was not a way unknown to them, as such ways were already common in the Polynesian Islands, which they had left before. Ironically, it is said that this was part of the reason they left their homeland to come here. Yet, once again they were convinced it would give them more power and so it was all over the world then. Today we still sacrifice, but it is hidden in all kinds of modern ways.'

'Yes, this is so, but does it really have to continue this way?' I found that tears were springing to my eyes.

'I have been praying here for years, performing the rites so that Ku will stay his hand in the face of both human innocence and foolishness. I pray for our people that we may be preserved, if not in the complete pureness of our blood but in the pureness of our spirit that has mingled with the blood of so many lands. What is it that you think you can accomplish here in Hawaii or at this place in particular?' With this, the *kahuna* pointed at the *heiau*.

'I'm asking for guidance as to where to put my offering. Then I need to know where to go next because I'm asking the gods to help us do matters differently this time, so that we don't destroy ourselves again by still appeasing the God of War, the one who lusts for conquest and blood instead of creation and love of life. To help us to grow inside emotionally and spiritually. We can't change ourselves until we change the way we do things, and the gods will not change unless we do. Victor said that we are partners with the gods, whether either we or they like it or not. Something has to stir and change for the better.'

'And that would be an act great of magic indeed,' the *kahuna* responded, pausing for a moment before continuing. 'You should make your offering at another *heiau* up the dirt road right by the coast. Be very respectful there; it is very old, and tourists do not go there. Go first to the little house and see if the caretaker is there. If not, follow your heart.'

'Thank you,' I replied. 'We passed by that house on the way up here and I felt drawn to it. Still, I would love to see the inside of this *heiau*. I feel, after all, that even if you disagree with a person or god somewhat, it doesn't mean you can't be respectful, you know.'

She smiled a little. 'Yes, that is true, but please don't climb the rocks and...' She stopped herself. 'Excuse me. Of course, you would not climb on the rocks. It's just that I've been surprised by supposedly educated people. A professor once climbed them without even asking, directly in front of me. I thought he would know better, but was I wrong.' She sighed.

'My friend and I would never be so rude and, besides, I've been watching all the birds. Even they seem reluctant to land on the *heiau*. That alone tells me something.' I laughed.

The *kahuna* laughed for the first time. 'Well, I will not say that they never land there, but they do so carefully. Most people would not even notice such a thing.' She nodded approvingly. 'I wish you and your friend good luck and my offer with you still stands. Just find me.' She gave me a warm bright smile and walked away with her attendants, none of them looking back.

The whales were heading further out to sea and Linda was returning up path. The sun was getting lower, and from this I knew we had just enough time to get to the other *heiau* after taking a peek of this one. We walked into the enclosure. It was dark and imposing, even with the blue-sky overhead.

'Do you wonder that maybe because gods like these are not being directly worshipped in the way they were in times past, that somehow we're being egged on and tricked into spilling blood for them anyway?' mused Linda.

'That is a terrible and cruel idea,' I responded quickly. 'As far as I know, many of the ancient gods of war had their codes of honor. They didn't revel in death but in causes and acts of heroism. They were in accord with the realization that battle was a part of the cycle of life. War could be an act of survival for many different reasons, not simply entertainment for the gods or to demonstrate their power over humankind.'

'Sure, I can see that, but I also see thousands of years of war and death as a kind of worship, from India through the Middle East and parts of Africa and eastern Europe through Russia.' Linda drew in the sand with her toe. 'Lots of time, land, and people, if you believe in the reincarnation thing, doing it over and over. No wonder they wanted religions that said you just go to heaven or hell.'

'It's a lot to think about, that's for sure,' I answered.

We walked into the impressive structure and looked around. The altar had handmade objects and flowers on it, but we did not approach it closely.

'Ku still has his respect and dignity in this place and a

loyal priestess,' I remarked. 'Maybe this god appreciates and understands more then we know.'

The enclosure became more shadowed as the sun was starting to go down and we needed to go to the other *heiau* before it set. We took our leave quickly and respectfully.

Hopping back into the car, we made our way back down the road and pulled into a small driveway by the older *heiau*. We gathered together the flowers we had picked earlier, fruit we had brought along and a few small crystals. At first it was not clear where to enter the *heiau*, but I remembered the *kahuna*'s instructions, so we went first up to the little house just a few steps away and knocked on the door. There was no one home.

'It's just sort of spooky and profound that here we are, and the place is all cleared out except for a *kahuna* you've now come to know,' stated Linda.

'Yeah, I know what you mean. Since no one is here, I guess we're on our own. After all, the *kahuna* said I should follow my gut. I think I see now where we can go in.' I nodded in the general direction and we started back.

We took a path to a wooden gate that was a little higher than our waists between the high stone walls. The minute I touched the gate I felt an energy that was remarkably like the tingling of an electrical current although there were no wires or metal to conduct such a current. Linda felt it as well.

'I don't know if going in is such a good idea.' She frowned.

'I believe this gate has a spell on it, one that makes you think twice about what you're doing here and that you'd better enter with good heart and clear intention. I need to go in, and I think it will be just like the other gate,' I responded with some confidence.

Indeed, there was more than one latch, but all opened easily. Linda walked along the outside of the walls. They were so much lower than the walls of the other *heiau*, only waist high, and it made me wonder if it was designed for rites and prayers at sunrise and sunset. We paused and

Linda helped me make sure we had not forgotten anything as once again we put together an offering. She then watched me while I found my way toward what seemed to be the altar in the middle of the structure. As I walked, I realized that this was shaped to be a small labyrinth. When I reached the altar, there were fading flowers of various kinds, leaves for *leis,* along with the remains of *taro* and fruits placed there, with which nature and the birds had their way. This is where I placed our offerings as well, then I closed my eyes. It is hard to describe the feeling of peace and love that so quickly overcame me, and as I started talking and praying to the gods, I thought of Lono and I visualized Victor's face and different parts of our journey, along with the signs and omens that had brought us here. I, somehow, was given the impression that Lono had a lot to do with this *heiau,* so I acknowledged the feeling and then greeted Uli and Pele as well. I told them about my conversation with the *kahuna* and asked sincerely for instructions concerning what to do next and a sign to confirm that I had it right.

A thought, accompanied with an inner vision, jumped into my mind. It surprised me. *Is this right*? I thought to myself. *Is this really where we need to go?*

I opened my eyes to see the sun setting directly in front of the altar before me. Its fiery ball was just touching the sea, surrounded by an array of beautiful sunset colors. As I was taking all this in, a large black dolphin leapt out of the sea and jumped over the setting sun in a perfect arch. It took my breath away; my heart in my throat from sheer wonder and excitement.

'Did you see that?' Linda called, almost shouting. 'It was perfect! Like it was a sign or something!'

'It was!' I called to her with identical force. I thanked the gods and carefully closed the gate behind me.

'We need to hot foot it back, because we have a bit of a trip ahead of us,' I informed her.

'Oh, yeah? And where are we off to now?' Linda asked.

'We are off to a very high volcano and it's going to be pretty chilly. This will be the last place to make an offering and then, as far as I know, our job is done. We have to be there at the very top by no later than ten tomorrow night.

'So, we'll be doing this at night on the top of a volcanic mountain that still might have snow on it?' Linda queried.

'Yeah... That could be about right,' I replied, as I gathered up our things.

'Well,' Linda responded, 'we better get going, then, because it's a long ride there and a long way up. If we get going now and get some sleep, we'll be there by tomorrow night and not be too exhausted.'

We were quiet on the way back, but our hearts sang.

Part IX

Prayers, Prophecies and Promises

After sleeping at our little hotel, we awakened at an early hour the next day. We called Victor, who suggested we might visit some gardens and peaceful places before heading up the mountain. We took his advice and found the local garden park stunning. We walked through, taking in the heady scents of plumier flowers mixed with many other floral scents. We enjoyed the beautiful and unusual tropical trees and, of course, the breathtaking orchids.

Linda, however, was a little impatient to get off the beaten path, so we left the town behind and headed toward the mountain. It was around eleven when we pulled up by an old service road to check our map.

'This looks kind of interesting. Let's explore.'

Agreeing, we headed up a short way to a little pullover spot. From there was a narrow path-like road that headed up the side of a wet hill that was so steep we had to climb it more then walk.

'Let's see what's up there,' suggested Linda.

'I have a dress on,' I replied, not really relishing what looked like a fairly arduous climb. Still, from somewhere came a strange pull.

Linda chuckled, 'Since when has that ever stopped you?'

Laughing and rolling my eyes, I once again pulled the back of my maxi dress between my legs. However, since I was not wearing a bra, I bit down on the hem and started climbing, at points grabbing small trees and roots to pull myself up. My muffled grumbling was barely heard all the way.

Linda scampered by and was quickly above me. 'I think this levels out pretty fast,' she encouraged.

Soon we were at the top, both panting slightly. We were on a service road of some kind that was used just enough to keep the underbrush down, but not enough to kill it. Large trees were growing on either side, junglelike, and birds were singing everywhere: all this with no sound of traffic, planes or people.

'It's quite lovely here. I'm glad we climbed up,' I uttered, a little sheepishly. 'Let's walk a little.'

Before taking everything else in and walking on, Linda and I took stock of our surroundings, so we would not forget the opening we had popped out of in the brush. It was so… green and the sky so blue and clear. On one side of us rose a little rocky cliff, at most eight or so feet high. Some wires stretched overhead, most likely the reason for the road. We had not gone far when a flash of color in the cliffside caught our eyes. There was a round hole around three feet up from the ground and about the size of a large dinner plate. It was filled in with paste-like earth that was brick red in color. Traces of it snaked down into the road, apparently whenever it rained, leaving little rivulets of red staining the ground

'Wow,' I said, when I realized what it was; 'that's natural red ocher like what they paint the old petroglyphs with.'

'Didn't they paint themselves with it? Kind of like the American Indians or the people from the South Seas do?' Linda asked.

'Victor mentioned how the people of the world paint themselves, but now that I think about it, many of the *tikis* (the lava statues of the gods) have what look like face paint or tattoo type marks on them. And I've seen dancers from many south sea lands use black, red and white body paint. There's a gold and yellow that's also used, but that's more in New Guinea, I think. Certainly, with it being here and people using it to draw with, it would also make sense to use it on themselves.'

'Then maybe we should put it to use. After all, it was just so random that we came up here, and here is this ceremonial stuff just presenting itself.'

'That's true, Linda, but we don't have anything to carry it in.'

'Who said anything about carrying anything with or in...?' Linda picked up some of the red clay by the end of her finger. 'How about on?'

I stared at Linda's fingertip and her idea came to my mind. 'How about we paint ourselves and ask the Gods for protection and blessing as we go up the mountain to make our last offering tonight?'

'Sounds like a great idea. How do we do this?' asked Linda, finger still poised.

I dipped my finger into the earth ochre pot. 'The only honest way we can. We're not Hawaiian and using symbols from other traditions would not be appropriate, but we can mark ourselves with the red earth of Hawaii to honor the land and the volcano and to appeal for their advice and blessing.'

We painted each other with simple lines and a few dots on our arms and faces. Then I said a prayer. Linda, who always had her handy pouch on her belt, had an extra stone crystal that she hid in the stones accompanying the ochre pot on the cliff. We stared at the red ochre for a silent minute. We each had the identical thought that this was like an open vein of the earth that had been revealed when the road was cut. Satisfied, and glad we had followed what seemed like a whim, we returned to the opening that would take us back to the car.

We soon realized that it was going to be harder climbing down than it had been going up. My faithful Doctor Scholl's wooden shoes would not be of any help either. Both of us looked for and found strong sticks we could use as canes, and I slipped my shoes into the sling of my dress, once again putting its hem in my mouth. The ground was steep, moist and slippery. Linda had her sturdy hiking shoes on, so she got down more easily. Between using a stick and grabbing onto what I could, I managed to walk and at times slither down the hill.

By the time we got to the car both of us were quite the sight, especially me. We laughed at each other and I suggested that we find a spring or river where we could clean up and change clothes.

After driving up the road for around ten minutes, we came to a river, where there was a large picnic space with thick shady overhanging trees. This must be a local park of some kind. A large family, with several young children and a few pre-teen kids, were playing in the river, while women were cooking, the men were tending a pit roast in the ground. The elderly were merrily speaking amongst themselves while keeping their eyes on a toddler. From the look of the people, I guessed they were Hawaiian and

Philippine for the most part. We pulled up a little downriver and started to rinse the dirt off our feet, legs, faces and arms. This only seemed to make the red ocher stain brighter on our skin. I told Linda that I would go see if the people had some soap because that might help. When I approached the family, they smiled and waved.

I felt a little embarrassed, but managed to say to the closest women;

'I know that we must look like some crazy *haolis* but we found a pot of red ocher in the ground and used it to say some prayers to the spirits of Hawaii to thank them for the wonderful time we were having.'

One of the men approached us, laughter bubbling up in his eyes.

'If that was the only type of crazy, we have to witness from outsiders it would be a blessing. Now, have you seen the petroglyphs?'

'Just the pictures around the visitor centers,' I replied.

'Then you're aware that they're hundreds of years old maybe much more. That red ocher sticks around,' he said pointedly.

The look of horror on my face must have been priceless.

The women reached out and slapped the man on his arm. 'You overgrown boy!' she said in mock anger. 'Trying to frighten this poor girl.'

The man only laughed harder as Linda approached.

'What's so funny?' she asked.

'Looks like we might be marked up for a while,' I told her.

'I may be able to help a little,' said the kind woman. She reached into a big woven straw bag and pulled out a jar of Pond's Cold Cream. 'Put on a thick layer and go stand in the sun. Let it warm up and then rub it off.'

We did this and could only laugh at ourselves when one of the children asked us if we had been wanting to play cowboys and Indians like on TV. When we felt our skin was warmed enough, the women gave us paper towels and, to my relief, some cold (now warm) cream did lift some of the red off, but it was still visible.

'Do not worry,' beamed the woman. 'If you need to go somewhere it will blend in with a little make-up.'

'Oh, we're not worried. We're just going to the top of the mountain tonight,' Linda replied.

'More prayers?' asked the man, raising his eyebrows with a humorous tone to his voice.

'Yup,' answered Linda quite simply.

'Halley's Comet is making its last close pass tonight, so we hope we can see it,' I added

'You see!' The woman slapped the man's arm again. 'These are serious girls. They pray! You might do that now and then! Come,' she said, herding us to the picnic table heavily laden with food. 'There is more than enough for everyone.'

The next hour and a half were full of laughter, stories, and good food. When we left, we were given some packed food to take with us. We gave hearty *mahalos* and *alohas* and left with full stomachs and full hearts.

Now, Hawaii showed us another one of her many faces once more. As we climbed slowly up the mountain, parts of this land seemed like a desert on another planet, with strange-looking plants I had never seen before. As we got higher up the volcano, there were Pele's trees, with their fire red flowers, growing in between old lava flows. Every few miles or so, we would pause to take in the breathtaking vistas. As we rose higher and higher toward its peak, it was somewhat astonishing to us that something so large just grew up in the middle of such a huge ocean, so many miles away from other lands.

As we reached the very top there were a few patches of melting snow and a chill in the air, but it was not as cold as I expected it to be. The sun was setting, making the views even more spectacular. There was a large parking lot with a few cars and a tourist bus that was getting ready to leave.

There also was the very well-known observatory not far away, which was only logical because the skies here were so clear. We decide to scout out the crater, which to our amazement, was unbelievably huge. It was also not a sudden drop into a hole like many other volcanos but a long, long, sloping gradual drop.

'Gods!' cried Linda. 'Looks like this has been a long dormant volcano. Whatever you end up doing tonight, we're not coming out here without a flashlight. One stumble and that would be a long roll to forever before you ever hit bottom.'

I agreed, and we continued to wander about.

After a while, Linda remarked 'I really think that even though it doesn't look like this is a camping spot, we should set up the tent anyway.'

'Why is that?' I asked.

'Because as soon as the sun sets it will get colder,' answered Linda in her most sensible tone. 'And if anything, unusual happens – which is almost guaranteed – you might need a place to lie down, and frankly I don't want to freeze my tail off on our last night in Hawaii.'

'Sounds good to me,' I agreed.

We went back to the car, grabbed our tent, and set up with some difficulty on the very hard rocky soil. There was a ranger or research station nearby, but no jeeps or cars near it. Still, we prudently pitched the tent as best we could in this wide-open space, at a slight angle, by a small rock pile. Linda brought some heavier items from the car and set them at the back of the tent, muttering to herself that she was not going to be blown into some damn crater in the middle of the night. This made me chuckle.

Once satisfied with our comfort and safety, Linda turned to me and said, 'Ok, out with it.'

'Out with what?' I answered back, somewhat surprised.

'Out with the whole story of why we're here. Don't tell me that we're just passing a howdy-do from Victor to the Gods! There's more to it than that and you've been dancing around it the whole trip. I think I've earned the right to know, even if I'm not one of Victor's disciples.' She crossed her arms over her chest and gave me a " you aren't going anywhere till I get my answers" look.

'Yes, you're right. There *is* more to it, but I thought if I didn't lay it all out at once it wouldn't be so overwhelming and things would just come together, which they did and have.'

'Yes, they sure have, and it's been one hell of a cool ride on one hand.' Linda smiled. 'But on the other hand, I'm still not hearing a clear answer as to why we're up on top of a freezing volcano in the middle of the night and not on some nice warm beach somewhere, flirting with the locals.'

I paused, taking a deep breath. 'A few months ago,' I began, 'I had this vision and these strange dreams. They somehow all seemed to point to this particular time that coincided with the coming of Halley's Comet.'

'I thought that comet had been around for a while,' questioned Linda, furrowing her brow.

'Yes, it has,' I continued. 'Different parts of the earth have seen it at different angles, but it is tonight that it makes its last, and closest, pass to the earth. I spoke to Victor regarding these things. He explained that we are in a very important time in human history and that humanity has to wake and "step up to the plate" so to speak, by facing all the good and bad of this world. All of humanity needs to make some sound and logical spiritual decisions. He said that just making the choice in our own hearts and in our prayers would only be fifty percent of the battle. Another twenty-five percent would be the willingness of people to get their hands dirty in whatever way suits them to clean up this world, and the final twenty-five percent is the willingness to stand up for what is right, no matter what your cultural or religious affiliations are, and to just say no to cruelty, greed, injustice, oppression, and enslavement in all its forms. We have to say yes to life, to love, to spiritual enlightenment. Say yes to all the things that make life worth living, instead of standing helpless as the evil in this world wraps us in sugar-coated lies, so we become frozen with doubt, waiting to be gobbled up.'

'Ohhh-kay.... So, what are you going to do about it?' asked Linda.

'Well... I've already started doing something before we even left San Francisco. You see, because of all the things I do, I know lots of people who live and travel all over the world, so I made a bunch of phone calls and at 11:00 tonight, as the comet comes into view, there'll be all these people, from rock musicians on tour, to the people from my church and all the pagans I know, all praying for us, and for all the people of this world. They will be praying for peace, for growth, for the opening of hearts and the strength to turn the tide that is leading toward chaos and destruction. They will appeal for wisdom, help, and time.

'Time? What do you mean time?' asked Linda.

'The time that we are running out of,' I replied seriously. 'You know me, Linda. I'm not a doomsday person, nor do I think that the apocalypse is around every corner, just because sometimes things look crazy and there's a lot to be depressed about, if you really give it any adequate thought. But it was part of my vision of how things are unfolding, that if we don't ask for spiritual help, it is all going to get really ugly much sooner rather than later.'

'So, what do you need to be doing right now?' Linda asked, manifesting her practical side.

'I need to practice my Hawaiian and meditate, clear my head,' I answered.

'Ok, the sun is starting to go down. We need light and warm food. You might also think about getting a little rest.' And with that Linda went into action.

The next few hours passed by quietly and peacefully. Occasionally, we heard cars come and go and voices in the distance.

Sometime between 10:30 to a quarter to 11 p.m. we came out of our tent. It was pitch black, and the chilly night air was surprisingly filled with what we figured was the singing of thousands of crickets. No other person was anywhere in sight. We made our way to the edge of the crater, trying not to get too close to its downward dip, to find a secure place to stand. Linda turned off the light and was going to let me know when it was exactly 11 by her watch. I picked up our offerings when suddenly there was total silence. The crickets had stopped singing at exactly 11 p.m. Linda raised her eyebrows at me as if to say there's your cue.

So, I began.

It felt as if I was standing at the edge of space. As soon as my eyes adjusted to the darkness, we were surrounded by stars. I started to say my Hawaiian prayers, my voice echoing in the belly of the volcano. I took four deep breaths, centered myself, said the flower prayer and threw the offerings as far out into the crater as I could. I listened for the sound of impact and rolling. Instead this starry blanket wrapped itself around me. At first, all I could see was that I was surrounded by this dizzying star-speckled darkness. I felt warmed all over, as if I were standing naked under a perfect sun. A voice came out of the starry darkness, having the warmth and comfort of sand and soil, the sharpness of metal and minerals, the strength and beauty of shining brilliant jewels. I was in the presence of something, or someone, that was very powerful and divine in nature. I could not move; I felt that I was floating now in the sparkling darkness all about me. I could not see Linda. I could only manage to find my wits to say: 'Victor sends his greeting.'

'Victor has been greeting us very well all over these islands.' I heard amusement in the golden tones filling my head, amusement that was decidedly feminine. I wondered, in the back of my mind, if this was Pele or Uli or perhaps something far older. Another thought hit me like a gentle wave; 'We are well pleased with our priest and *kahuna* and touched by you and your friend's kindness and courage.'

My heart welled and, somehow, I realized that the warmth I felt was a physical manifestation of love, as my head filled with her words. I answered back aloud.

'Thank you for all your help and guidance on this journey. Yet, what we are seeking help and praying for, seems so overwhelming and so much to ask for, even of a goddess or a god.'

'What is it that you wish above all things?' The voice asked.

'That we…. humankind…. be given a chance and time to grow a little more, to help us to see all the beauty in the world, and in ourselves, that is so worth living for. To be able to awaken ourselves somehow from self-imposed limitations, to not be afraid to live up to what is divine in us.'

I found myself somewhat in a pleading mode, but I wasn't totally sure why my words made me so emotional, other than this deep stirring within me that compelled me to ask, 'Is it true, Divine One, that we have run out of time, as so many say and preach?'

There was a pause of meaning and depth, precisely like the pause in great music. I felt as if I were made of clear glass and that there was no part of me that was not exposed to this Being.

'Every point in history whether it is in the past, your present or the future is caused mostly by the hearts, voices and deeds of humankind with a few mitigating factors. There are cold, lost human hearts that control much of this earth. Some are influenced by forces larger than themselves, yet many are motivated only by their own filth that has stained and twisted their heart and mind, sometimes tragically, their very souls. In truth, there are few fully trained warriors, as well as awakened ones, to champion the cause of the just and to stand against this tide at this time. This has afforded the masses of humanity an illusion that evil prevails. The emotional and spiritual body of this world is out of balance and seeks to right itself from the blasphemy and pollution that humankind has allowed. Yes, we are at a point of choice and, at a particular moment, that choice will result in a great war. So, it has gone for untold generations in this world.'

'Then please help us!' I pleaded. 'Such is not my choice, nor is it the choice of my friends. At this very moment so many are praying for a better future all over the world, so please share this moment with us as the choice of the innocent and of all creatures of earth that have a right to exist and evolve.'

There was a pause. I felt suspended in time and space, and that space glittered deep indigo blue and purple with flashes of tiny bright diamond-like stars.

The voice resumed. 'You must understand that everything has its cycle, its own life, its own laws to live by, be it people, nations, animals, storms and stars. Yet, for the sake of all your prayers of hope, for the sake of the faith of my priest, the gift of time this is what you will be given: What could have come to pass from this moment on shall not be. Instead, it will only be the warning and shadow of what could be. And this moment will rise again in five years.'

'Five years is such a short time!' I protested, boldly and emotionally. 'Think of all the music, movies and stories that will never be told. These stories that could open people's hearts, we need at least three times as much time, if not four or five,' I said sadly.

'Humankind has had all the time in the universe but that is something you cannot easily understand. If all goes well, then every five or so years humanity will be tested, and until fifteen years have passed, along the way the signs will grow, and the gods of nature will show their hand as humankind plays its part for good and ill. In fifteen years, we shall see if your bought time will be enough to bare the evils of your world for everyone to see. Then, by twenty-five years, we shall see if humanity's spirit will wake and work for its better tomorrow. Now that you have bought time from a goddess, what do you wish to see?'

'I wish to see people waking up. I wish to see that we will not be allowed to destroy ourselves this time, but that we have to clean up our messes and grow, so we will not be able to stand the sight of suffering and injustice. I wish for spiritual courage for all people and the power to change for the better, so we may come to understand who we really are and become the stewards of this earth as we were meant to be.'

'That is the long-held wish of many on both sides of the veil and stars. Remember, five years, ten and fifteen, then more tests and signs will come every five years till it be your future....'

'And at the end of twenty-five years, what will happen then?' I broke in, not able to help myself.

'Then humanity and We will decide which path it will tread, as it has always been. You now will have one last sign and revelation here, so that you do not doubt either your vision, or this work which has been completed.'

Before I could say anything, even a good-bye, a cold breeze brushed my face and the stars of the night revealed themselves again. I started to hear the slow and cautious chirps of the crickets as they slowly resumed their loud chorus. I was shivering and tingling all over.

'What time is it?' I asked Linda

'Oh, it's about a quarter past eleven, give or take a few,' she said.

'You're kidding! I thought I was out much longer than that!' I exclaimed. 'Did you hear my side of the conversation?'

Linda put her arms around me, because I was shivering. 'Out? Out where?' she asked. 'You did your Hawaiian prayers; threw the offering and you got all quiet. I thought you were praying silently, so I just waited.'

'Someone spoke to me. I think it was a goddess.'

'You didn't ask her name?' said Linda, a little shocked.

'Well, we got down to business kind of fast.' I started to look up toward the sky, turning about so that Linda let go of me.

'What are you doing?' Linda laughed.

'I'm looking for a sign. She said there would be a sign.'

'Well, it looks like you may be looking in the wrong direction.' Linda pointed.

I looked to where she was pointing with the flashlight. Then she turned it off. There in the distance far below, winding its way up the mountainside, was a long snake of yellow golden lights with flashes of bright red here and there. It was beautiful to see.

'What is it? It can't be cars, can it?' I asked aloud.

'Sure, seems to be that way. Looks like hundreds of them and they are heading straight for us. They should be here by midnight, I'd say. I guess your goddess had it all timed out. We did your thing and now it's party time,' grinned Linda.

Soon, the whole top of the mountain was filled with the laughing voices of children. There must have been close to several hundred kids of all ages from all over the island. We discovered that they were here to look at the comet as part of a school assignment. Trucks arrived with telescopes of all sizes, tailgates came down, food and drinks were offered and passed around. Soon there was singing, everything from Hawaiian songs, to folk tunes, to rock from car radios. Telescopes were shared and we all got a glance at Halley's Comet, a fuzzy little cotton ball with a little bit of neon blue around it. Linda and I had a wonderful time, and it was not until the wee hours that we crawled exhausted into our tent.

We were awakened by a ranger calling out to us at the door of our tent.

'Come on, sleeping beauties, I let you sleep as long as I could. I know last night was a special night, but you're not supposed to camp out here, you know.'

'Sorry officer, but we were so tired,' we said apologetically.

The officer laughed at us good-naturedly. 'Well, you're just lucky that my boss is down at headquarters listening to all the live news that has been going on all morning,'

'News? What news?' I asked, as I zipped open the tent flap to see the ranger's kind face.

'Oh, some sort of nonsense in the Middle East, somewhere in Libya. Christ! What is it they want to do? Start World War III?' he answered with disgust. 'They were trying to kill that Gaddafi guy, but something went wrong with the missiles. They didn't hit where they wanted them to, they said the missiles went all crazy, so they missed him. Still, they say that some people died including a baby. So tragic. Thankfully though, it looks like it may settle down for now. What could be the point of such a move?' He sighed. 'Anyway, my boss will be up fairly soon. So, up and at 'em, girls.' He prodded us encouragingly with these words .

As he walked away, I turned to Linda with big eyes and asked her, 'Do you know what could have happened if they had killed him? It might have ballooned to World War III.'

Linda seemed unfazed and looked at her watch. 'We've got a late flight out of here. What you say we get off this burg and head toward the beach?'

'Sounds like a plan,' I grinned.

And so, it was.

Original Epilogue

Victor was very happy to see me on my return. We spoke for many hours about Hawaii. I gave him back the well-worn slip of paper.

'We have done wellm,' he chuckled. 'My heart is lighter than it has been in a long time, even though it is still heavy with the knowledge that I will not see my beloved Hawaii in this lifetime. Still, much can be accomplished in the next twenty or more years.

'I want to write it all down, Victor.'

'And you shall, but not now,' he answered. 'It is not time. Things must unfold as they should.'

'But Victor, If I don't tell it now, people may not believe me after the fact,' I pled.

'Is it your wish to be the next Nostradamus? Or are you doing the work?' Victor asked me a little sharply.

'I was not even thinking about fame,' I said. 'I was thinking about how cynical people are and how they always need proof.'

'So it has been since the beginning of time. Besides, all the proof in the world will not move a closed heart,' said Victor, rocking in his chair. 'Think of all the tales of wisdom, the stories and legends that move us. Are they not true? In spirit if not in fact; even our most sacred texts were often written long after the fact. So, fear not.' He smiled. 'It will write itself when it is time.'

Victor was right. So, (other than writing a few paragraphs, notes and my pictures), I lived my life while Hawaii changed and grew herself. Pele added acres of land mass and coastline. Since 1986, I have sung professionally, helped put together non-profits and raised a child. Linda and I fell out of touch as she became a lawyer, married and built her own park around her home. Ten years have passed since I last spoke to Linda. I was writing the last chapter of this book, when the phone rang – and guess who was at my door before I knew it! What a surprise and a good omen. Linda and I had two happy days together, and I was very relieved that she loved the story and reminded me of a few things I had forgotten, which someday I will add to it.

On the last evening I spoke to Victor (in person not on the phone), he said to me, 'It is time to be strong because there will be hardship. Speak your truth.'

In the telling of this adventure I was vague about certain places, and the names of people, for the reason of privacy and safety for places as well as people.. This is also the reason that I changed the sequence of a few events. Still, this is how the story wanted and needed to be told.

New Epilogue

This year it has been 33 years since our Journey. In the years after, I learned so many things about Victor. Some of this information can be found in my book of interviews: *Victor Anderson: an American Shaman*. He told me that he could remember many lives and that he had been a priest, shaman, and/or medicine person in most of them. In others he was a martial arts teacher, musician or scientist, and in a few, a tribal leader. He told me of lives in Africa and various places in Europe, such as Ireland and Greece, India, Russia, Japan, Tahiti, up and down the Americas, especially Mexico and with the Northern Native tribes, but it was Hawaii that his heart cried for. Victor informed me that he had lived at least four lives in Hawaii, and that this was where he spent his life immediately previous to this one. It was one of Victor's great sorrows to know that, in this current life, he would never be able to go there physically. Victor told me, however, that he could and would spirit travel there, because as a young child, a toddler between two or three years of age, this psychic gift was awakened in him by various native people living in his area of New Mexico. They had taken him and laid him on a stone altar to pray for his health, and that his sight might be restored. Some of it was for, on a good day, Victor could see a little more, then mostly shadows. With a very bright light and a large magnifying lens he could read but it tired him, so he also relied on braille or listened to audio books. However, Victor's astral sight was fully awakened and with this he saw very well into the heart of our reality and into other realms of existence as well.

The time I spent with Victor helped me understand, and put into proper place, the separate bits of my heritage and life experience. I came to understand my own spiritual microcosm, coming to realize everything that lives encompasses the cells of a greater whole. Our awareness of this manifests according to our spiritual and psychic development and needs. The symbol of the rainbow hints at this wisdom and is partly why the rainbow represents a symbol of promise and fulfillment in so many cultures. The rainbow became the bridge, or great bow of the gods, the tool and symbol of how the Great Spirit paints our reality. Now, in our modern times it has become the symbol of the unity of the oppressed and is held aloft as a banner of hope.

We have been afforded a tremendous amount by our Earth. There's so much resource, beauty and time to create the lives and culture we want to experience. Yet, as the millennia have slipped by us, time and time again we become mentally entangled and morally confused, falling from common sense, discernment and mercy, to allow forces that seem out of our control to take us to the depths of cruelty, despair and suffering and ultimately to destruction and obliteration. Like abused children, we believe that this is meant to be for our own good.

This time we *can* live a different life. This time we *can* raise our bowed heads and drop our shame and guilt like the filthy second skin it has become. At that point, we can fully come to understand why the five petaled flower, the seeds in the apple, and Leonardo's human star are all a part of the sacred blueprint for this reality – and even this universe – according to Victor. The basis of mathematics, architecture, science, music, and medicine are all reflected in the human body itself. The common man, by observation, has seen and learned from these patterns, from the Stone Age to today. Though the people on this earth live under so many conditions, from the very isolated and simple to the very complex, in this modern age, all of us are reaching toward the stars and greater awareness, each in our own way.

Yet, here we are, once again coming perilously close to an unbelievable number of ways we could destroy ourselves and ruin this world for years to come. At this very moment in 2019, innocents still die in churches, mosques and temples in America and around the world. Yet despite this, the world has been so far spared the fall into the utter darkness of the abyss. Why? The fall that so many fear, and that could end all life, could have happened so easily several times in the past hundred years. Yet, today we still either blindly live on, or nervously wring our hands, waiting for the other proverbial shoe to drop. Is it possible that we are being denied our easy self-flagellating apocalypse because of, not just a few, but hundreds and thousands of prayers offered up, both on that night in 1986, and then by the great event of the Harmonic Convergence the following year?

The media all over the world did not just mention this phenomena, but filmed with wonder thousands of people, of every race and class, holding hands or individually praying, chanting, singing or standing in emotion-filled silence, and asking the Divine to help us find a better way. This was televised for days.

Since that time, some continue to maintain this prayer throughout various cultures around the globe. Do you really imagine - no matter how atheist, or secretly agnostic, in your heart of hearts you may be that no one has been listening? Did all these people think that this would not make a difference?

Think of all the choices, ideas, creations and movements in the face of resistance. Think of what changed, from people to governments, and the flow of events from then to now. Think of all the choices we have made as individuals, and as nations, since 1986. Yes, we made it through the attacks on September 11th, 2001 and after, but there is still so much work to do. So many issues, problems, injustices and even evil things to be resolved and changed.

We can do it. We *must* do it, or things will become, and remain, crushingly uncomfortable for us until we do.

I know some may not want to believe me, or perhaps do not take what I am writing and saying seriously. All I can say to those people is, please think again. Think of all the amazing amount of material online, from the sciences to our greatest poets. Even your local library is a storehouse of knowledge. Think of the wisdom of those who have risen to speak, from the traveling Grandmothers of various traditions, to those who have come down from the Himalayas. There are many more, such as native elders from both north and south America, sharing the words from their oral traditions. Think of our ancient sacred scripts, the stories and poetry that speak to our hearts in endless ways. Think of the movies and books that are so much more than just entertainment.

Science and educative knowledge are important, and of course a necessary part of human growth and survival, but we cannot rely on these alone and get very far in this prolific universe. We are destroying ourselves by holding onto this illusion. We also need the information and wisdom of spirit, and all the love that comes with it. We need to acknowledge and respect both the spiritual and the empirical, and what we achieve by giving them equal value. With the power of our intent and our intellect, our emotions can soar to such great heights of creativity. Through love, we have the power in our hands to heal ourselves and the mess we have allowed that has polluted our world. Our next five-year cycle begins in 2021. This year, in 2019, we have been told that we have two years to effect climate change enough so we will not be in a total climatic disaster within three to five years. We must clear our heads and become the men and women, with all our expressions of creation, to stabilize the great circle of life – no matter what skin tones, height, cultural and sexual expressions or how we otherwise might want to live our existence in the kaleidoscope of life. We are the means whereby possibility becomes reality. Let us not yet again be derailed by the illusions of greed, power and separateness the well-used tools of evil intent to confuse us and tempt us into selfish and destructive behavior.

We must realize that to create and to heal is to live and grow, not just as humans but as souls. This is our birthright, our joy, our purpose, no matter who we are or where we came from.

Before the Journey
A Conversation with Victor

Victor was sitting quietly in his rocking chair, making me nervous.

'So, what aspect of Mari is Pele?' I had just asked him the question. A sensible one, I thought.

'What ASS-pect might you think?' he said somewhat cynically. 'What does that even mean, hmmm?'

'Is it not like a part of something, or how things are positioned in relation to each other?' I answered. 'Like in astrology?'

'Yes, but it is also how things *might* appear. So, what aspect of Mari are we talking about here? Mari's left big toe to Pele's right pinky?

'Victor!' I laughed. 'We are not really talking physical here.'

'It can be on one hand; it's all how you look at it sometimes, but it can just as easily be all bullshit. *Aspect*. At times I really hate that word,' he grumbled.

'Victor, when we first met in person one of the first goddess names you told me about was Tonantzin because of the Mexican Indian in me.'

'Yes,' he said, nodding, 'and she may bear many names; Mother Earth, our Goddess of Corn and Plenty, Snake Mother of Wisdom, and our Mother of Love: all can be called Tonantzin.'

'So, she can also be seen as a love goddess, then?' I asked.

Victor sighed and paused. 'This should be something so obvious and simple. One of life's greatest joys. Yet, here on earth, sacred love itself has become so debased and degraded by our foolishness that it grew into a sexual complex so large it has degraded the power of love itself, so it is eating itself up like a snake eating its tail. We will destroy ourselves and most of life here if we do not wake up and stop it. Love is more than the beloved, be it lover or child. It is more than love of honor and devotion. It is more than family and community, though many have sacrificed out of love for such. It is more than adoration of pleasure and ecstasy though this too has its place among what is sacred. It is also the love of knowledge and wisdom, as it is the love of the scent of the rose on the wind. It is the love of the curl on the brow, the vision of birds and dolphins playing in the waves. We fall in love with the seashell that we spot in the sand, and the shocked puppy that sees snow for the first time. We fall in love under the moon and with The Moon. Love can be found everywhere and anywhere. We become truly alive in a state of love, for life itself is love and this is what we have forgotten.

'So, with this in mind Cornelia, see then that love becomes and is the honorific title added to "Our Lady" or "Our Great Mother". Some have claimed that, upon seeing the apparition of our lady upon the hill of Tepeyac, (where her temple had been destroyed), the native people immediately recognized the Lady of Guadalupe as their Tonantzin, for they recognized her love. She who emerges from light itself, like the Eagle Phoenix from fire. Such is the power of love and creation.'

'You told me that at that time,' I said, 'the Virgin Mary of Guadalupe was Tonantzin, that they are the same. That was why Mary made her appearance on the ruins of Tonantzin's temple that the Spaniards destroyed.'

'Yes, yes, very true.' Victor looked thoughtful for a moment. 'Remember when I spoke of the Divine Twins?'

'Yes, and that they pop up all over the world in myth and sacred tales. You also said something of twin flames, but we were on the phone at the time and I had to hang up.'

Victor squinted his eyes behind his thick lenses. 'I think over there on top of the bookshelf are some candle holders with candles still in them.'

I stood up and got them. Victor then directed me to another shelf containing a bowl that had pens, pencils and some matches. He now held the candle holders in front of him and said, 'Now, light them.'

As the candles sputtered to life and took a steady glow, he slowly started to bring the two candles closer together as he spoke.

'One of the reasons that life was so mysterious to humankind is because we could not comprehend all its mysteries. We had not yet invented microscopes and telescopes, or the various inventions that now enable us to peer into the macro and micro cosmos of the world around us. Even the sea, our next-door neighbor, was a frightening world where we could only skim its surface. So, it was through myth and sacred stories that wisdom and meaning were passed down to us. We learned from the geniuses and sages of old, from ancient developed cultures and from the gods themselves. So, be that as it may, here we have these two candles. Let us say the light blue one is Mary and the yellow one is Tonantzin. They are both two things and or two beings in each of my hands. Mary comes from the Middle East and Europe, while half a world away we have Tonantzin in the Americas, and even though they have different names, dress differently and are goddesses from different cultures, they are both contained in the same kind of vessel, like these candles. Both are a living flame, living energy that connects them to their people on earth.

'Now, these beings move closer together here on earth, through the movement of people, and they meet.' Here Victor brought the candle sticks together with a little click. 'And now two wonderful things happen: They recognize that they are of the same nature and...' Victor tilted the top of the two candles together until they were a seamless single flame, 'they become one and present themselves accordingly. We too see them as such, but by the influences of custom and the authority of man, they are dressed and addressed as we know them now. What is not so understood is that it is not so much the old and new becoming one, but a repackaging or renaming of what has always been there. Yet ...' he pulled the candles apart again, '...they can still present themselves as two beings or one.'

'Tonantzin and Mari are not Pele, then?'

'What do you think?' Victor asked before blowing out the candles.

I thought for a moment, then followed my gut. 'Even though there is a grandmother/mother side to Pele, and you used a flame to make your point, my instinct says not. From what you have told me before it would be more Uli and Mary and Tonantzin.'

He nodded. 'Now, you are using your head. Understanding the nature of the gods and goddesses is like understanding chemistry.'

'Yet, you have also said that all gods are Feri gods and ultimately we are all one.' My forehead must have been one big wrinkle as I tried to wrap my mind around these ideas and thoughts.

'We are all ultimately beings of light.... wave patterns of energy and minute particles we just barely know exist, let alone understand. These are the tools of the gods of nature. Tonantzin, Mother of Earth and Moon, her power the cycles of life, is united with the Virgin Mother Mary, who is also united with the moon and the stars and water, as Uli is the mother of magic and making. Still, because we do not understand magic to be a part of science and nature, we are suspicious of it, even fear it. Yet, it is a part of all the dimensions we come from. Instead, we've created superstitions and religions that often do not serve us in the way we wished or intended. In Feri, the gods are real people, not mere ideas or concepts. Where else do you think the Christians got the idea of a personal savior or the Trinity?'

'So, can there be three candles like the Father, Son and Holy Ghost being one and three, three and one?' My eyebrows raised.

'Well, in theory you could say that, but it's also somewhat a horse of a different color,' Victor chuckled.

'How so?'

'Think about it, Cornelia. What does the three symbolize?' he asked.

'The most obvious thing that comes to mind is Father, Mother and Child. For Christians it's the Father, Son and Holy Ghost representing the mystery of three as one.'

Victor nodded sagely. 'Yes, that is true. Now, let us widen the lens here for a moment. One of the reasons I love the teachings of the Hawaiian *kahuna* ways of looking at life and spirit is its practicality and basic understanding of how things really are. This is understood by most shamans and spiritually gifted people all over the world. The *kahuna* in Hawaii, the Native Americans and the aborigines in Australia, the druids of the British Isles. Early man's bottom line was, "All we know we stand on." And that was a hell of a lot more than we, in modern times, realize. They knew then that the earth, its waters and the air we walk in and through, are all a part of one world, and yet obviously each is its own world as well, filled with countless creatures. It was only logical to think, because of this, that the waters would have its own people – we call them mermen and mermaids. The air is moved by winds as water is by waves. Our skies are filled with birds and traveling stars filled with the consciousness of angels and diminutive spirits that here we call fairies. Remember that not all are small creatures some are quite large. Still, be that as it may, people always look for their own image everywhere to define intelligence, so they often miss intelligence and awareness, even when it is right under their nose. Still, ancient man managed to perceive that all the elements were each their own world. The air filled with wind and its own creatures that flew toward the heavens toward the home of the mysteries of spirit. Originally, fire was part of both air and earth for obvious reasons.'

'Really?'

'Use your noodle!' Victor stamped his cane on the floor. 'Work your nut!'

'Oh!' My cheeks turned red. 'Because of the sun!'

'Yes, go on…' he encouraged.

My thoughts were dashing about like a mouse in a maze. 'And of course, fiery meteors falling from the sky, which were thought to be falling stars.'

'Indeed, go on...'

'And lightning! Striking trees and fields and setting them afire.'

Victor nodded but was silent.

'And comets!' I added triumphantly. 'And now, that I am using my noodle,' I laughed, 'there is also the Northern Lights and other things that happen in the skies that we now call UFOs. Yet fire is also a part of earth, not just in flames, but in the center of volcanos and in the heat of the forge.'

'Very good.' Finally satisfied, Victor continued tracing a triangle on the floor with his white cane. 'Here we have the original Trinity, which as a symbol pointing up, means stability, strength and forward, upward or outward movement. With the point down it is grounded, contained, rooted stability. The upward tip is the dimension of where air, water and fire plays around us in this world as wind, rain and lightning, for example. The downward pointed triangle is a symbol of fire, water and air contained within the earth. Lava, gases, various fluids all beneath our feet. If you take the bottom of these two, even triangles and put them together, you now have a four-sided diamond shape with a line through it. The space inside the diamond shows our reality here in symbolic form. This is an ancient observation and teaching. Now, what happens when you pull the triangle shapes together on top of each other.

I closed my eyes for a second. 'You get a six-pointed star.'

'The downward pointing triangle is woman and the upward the man for obvious reasons. When they are joined, they are the four elements with the power of within and without, or above and below; the creative forces that house the spirit,' Victor chuckled. 'All stars have their meaning and secrets, but it is the six-pointed star that is the star of the power of humankind on this earth, while the five-pointed star is the star of the power of nature, and how man and womankind are a part of nature and its laws, not separate from it. Therefore, we find these shapes and designs all through nature and in our solar system and beyond. When we do not respect or understand this fundamental fact, chaos on all levels of our existence comes after us like the great Nothing in the book '*The Never-Ending Story*,' which is much more than a children's book, by the way'.

'When the missionaries and later, professors of various kinds, descended on Hawaii, they did not comprehend that the "primitive people" understood many subtle principles both philosophically as well as scientifically. How could they? They were hamstrung by their prejudices and arrogance and could not perceive that knowledge could be hidden not only in symbols, but in the poetic language of the Hawaiians themselves. That sometimes, a name was a descriptive, such as Saviour, Messiah, Lord – like all names we use for Jesus. Hina is known all over Polynesia; it is a very old name for the goddess. Laka and Kap'o are thought of as separate goddesses but they are not; they are simply other names of the qualities of our great goddess. In Tahiti, she is called Tawahine. When the ancestors of the Hawaiian people first came to the Hawaiian Islands, they mostly worshiped Tane and Wahine, which simply means man and woman as the Divine Pair. These are the oldest concepts of divinity,' he intoned. 'Though concept, is another word I have mixed feelings about. So, you see Cornelia, we had the trinity long before others did, and that does not mean I turn up my nose at how it is now depicted in churches and temples all over the world. It is just hard to see how this has come to be so hidden, misunderstood and reviled'.

'In certain prayers, and certainly at times I too refer to the goddess as Keakua Kanawahine Makua Hine O Mahoku, which means the god, male and female as the mother and father of the stars of heaven. For what you are about to do, you will address her as Uli, our loving breast and beloved mother.' Victor let out a great sigh and was silent a moment before speaking again. 'Even St. Paul in the Bible said that deep down men know the truth in their hearts. The people of North Africa and the Middle East deposed the ancient goddess in favor of the God of War, also known as the god of patriarchalism, who used any means necessary, besides battle, to conquer and oppress: rape, torture, starvation, humiliation, murder, amounting to complete desecration and destruction. This is not the God, the true male god, the son, brother and love of the Divine Shekhina, the female side of God. It is certainly is not the father of Jesus either. People need to wake up and understand what they are worshiping and giving their power to. If people say they believe in love and that God is love, then they had better know what that is.'

'Is that what this is ultimately all about Victor - God and Goddess calling out for us to remember all that love truly is?'

A big grin spread across Victor's face and filled the room. 'You could say that.'

(I'd like to mention here that interested readers might like to read Victor's classic work 'Etheric Anatomy', in which he spoke extensively about the triple nature of the soul.)

More About Hawaiian Ways

It is the Hawaiian *hula* that preserves so much of the ancient Polynesian religion. This sacred dance that is mostly slow and sensual, with graceful hand and arm movements, is Hawaii's special way of storytelling, for the movements are a language of their own.

People carried the dance with them as they came from Tahiti, Rarotonga, Samoa and the Cook Islands. Ancient Polynesian wisdom and traditions are hidden and preserved in the sacred *hula* dance. The songs, chants and rites of the *kahuna* are to remind the gods of nature that their people have not forgotten and to call them forth to celebrate and feast with them. It is a relationship of love and respect. It is in these times of sacred space that the *kahunas*, and the people of Hawaii, gain the necessary and essential moments of insight needed to penetrate through human blinders and see through the veils and touch upon the nature of divine love and wisdom. From this understanding, the gods pour out the tides of life, from first breath to last, from gain to loss, the in and out, the back and forth, that are the tides of all existence through space and time.

The *kahunas* of Hawaii were, and are, a web of knowledge, skills and awareness. Victor spoke of the science of life that the *kahunas* practiced; both men and women had their areas of specialty. Those who were exceptionally gifted could have more than one. In essence, they are experts. Victor told me that all those who gazed upon the stars around the world and carefully took note of their movements, as well as those who observed nature and experimented in order to learn to build and cook, were our first scientists and we owe them much. It is also why all around the world, words that apply to magic and science are often words that are also applied to cooking, to turn, bend or make new, also to see or walk through, to heal or make straight or flexible. Though the Polynesian Hawaiian language seems simple, it is precise, yet flexible, in ways that modern culture does not understand, so therefore does not give it the respect it deserves.

Victor would become outraged by the dismissal of the Polynesian people.

'These short-sighted fools do not understand the long ancient history of this planet, and if it were not for the courage and determination of those who traveled the seas, or lived hidden in mountains or hostile deserts, or on scattered islands, humankind may have never made it to this point.'

It amazes me that so many predictions from Victor about what the anthropological and archaeological worlds would discover after his passing, have been coming true, with new discoveries almost every day it seems. Many indeed are through the efforts of Andrew Collins, of whom Victor said after reading the book '*From the Ashes of Angels*'

'This man is figuring out the truths of our ancient past. He and his friends will open doors to knowledge that could really help humankind if they pay attention.'

I believe that the some of Andrew Collins' friends that Victor spoke of are the authors and explorers of history and mysteries; Graham Phillips, Gregory L Little and Graham Hancock. I like to think that they might agree with Victor, and that any great power and wisdom, as it weaves its way through our ages, can become weakened or corrupted. Great cities and nations rise and fall. Science and philosophies fade under the hammer of time, and what was once known becomes lost or hidden, till like a long-frozen seed it rises again. We become so blessed when we recognize the meaning of the tree of life. It is by not seeing ourselves as a part of it that we are left feeling so alone and hungry for meaning. When we allow it to grow again within us, its fruit hangs within our reach. This is the intelligence and inspiration that feeds the seeker and nourishes heroes to defend our home, to celebrate its creation, thereby bringing hope to all people. This is what we must remember. This is creation's thread that ties all humanity together throughout time. Victor knew, without a shadow of doubt, how this thread spun about our earth. Though many places and cultures held his body and mind it was Hawaii where he left his heart and its spirit called his soul.

Victor Speaks About *Huna*

For those that are not familiar with the term and spiritual practice called *huna,* and Victor's feelings about it, I will share a bit here.

The Hawaiian word was adopted by New Age author Max Freedom Long (1890–1971) in 1936 to describe his theory of Hawaiian spirituality, and what he felt was its religious and metaphysical thought. Long felt that the spiritual practices of the ancient Hawaiian *kahunas* (the priests and teachers in Hawaii) held the key to a better form of human religious practice; however, the system to many seemed to be mostly his own invention, with roots in British occult ideals and theosophy, rather than in traditional Hawaiian beliefs.

Much has been said about Max Freedom Long and *huna.* Victor told me that he had spoken with Max long ago. Max was one of many well-known people Victor had corresponded with by tape, letter and phone. I remember once, Victor was washing the dishes and the phone rang. I picked it up to hear it was a woman from Hawaii calling asking for guidance from Victor. It was in this way, when I occasionally picked up the phone for Victor, or was present when people called, that I found out these calls were from as far away as Tahiti or Ireland, Italy, France, Canada and all over the United States.

'How do people as far away as Tahiti hear of you, Victor?' I asked him.

He cracked a little smile and told me that there were many ways. He knew people who worked and taught the old island ways from when he was quite young, having met them when living in Oregon as a teen. These people came as a choir from Tahiti, sponsored by local churches to visit and perform in Oregon. Victor also had many friends who travelled, and they would call during their travels and introduce Victor to people by phone now and then. Friends would bring others to Victor and Cora's house. Victor, of course, also had what he called his old-fashioned ways in letter writing, (what the kids now call snail mail), and could astral travel his body when in deep meditation. If he needed to speak with someone, he would find a way to reach them. So, by all these means, he spoke to quite a few well-known people such as Max Freedom Long. He would speak with writers that wrote for Fate Magazine such as Richard Shaver, scientists of the day, and other well-known pagan personalities who consulted him for various reasons.

In my early days of exploring San Francisco's religious, spiritual and musical scenes, it was like being at the banquet table of the gods. Just like it seemed you could find any kind of food from all corners of the earth in the city, so could you find any religion, path, philosophy or style of music. Those who considered themselves kin, or at the very least respected each other, exchanged information, students or disciples and took to the cafes of choice to wax profound, holding up various traditions to scrutiny or admiration. San Francisco was also filled with lecture halls, clubs, shops and churches that had backrooms, or basement rooms, that were often used for workshops and lectures. Of course, there were also libraries. Here I found bustling white or blue haired little old ladies with their gentlemen friends, usually younger with exotic dark-eyed looks, or the single distinguished white bearded man with eyes that saw all but gave nothing away. They mingled with ageing hippies and the growing crowd of the young and rich. The older people had been moving the century forward in their heyday and in many ways still were. This too Victor and Cora became a part of. In these times, Max

Freedom Long stepped out with his ideas, as did Gurdjieff before him and many others, such as: Manly P. Hall, Aleister Crowley, Anne Besant, Helena Blavatsky, Krishnamurti, Rudolph Steiner, Yogananda and Dion Fortune. Just a few of the great metaphysicians, teachers and philosophers of their day. In many ways, Max Freedom Long and his *huna* was like a bridge between Victorian/Edwardian occult ideas and the New Age metaphysics, of which he is considered to be a part. He had lived in Hawaii from 1917 to 1931. In those years, he worked as an elementary school teacher, but soon became fascinated with Hawaiian beliefs and customs. It was not until he left Hawaii in 1936 that he wrote his first book and developed his tradition of *huna*. This was a cobbling together of what he had learned while on the islands, with his own studies, which came out of his own inner revelations and his esoteric interests. Now, there are those who might say he made it all up and that he was an appropriator of the worst kind. Victor did not feel this way, even though he also felt that Max had a flaw in his nature. He felt that Max had been vulnerable to people who passed themselves off as having authority or knowledge they did not have. He told me that he had spoken with Max extensively. After these conversations, he felt he understood him somewhat better.

'I am of the opinion now that Max did speak with some *kahunas* who opened up somewhat to him. Of course, they did not tell him the deep inner secrets of their tradition, but I believe they told him what they could feel comfortable with.'

'Why do you feel that way?' I asked.

'Because he was trying to solve a problem that I have had to wrestle with myself. It is the issue that all teachers, leaders, poets and priests must wrestle with. Can you think what that might be?' Victor asked.

I thought about this before I responded with:

'How to show that the truths of yesterday matter today? Or perhaps how can the wisdom of the past help the people of today find meaning and a better future?'

Victor nodded. 'That is close enough. This is a tough row to hoe, Cornelia, because it is complicated and, in some ways, convoluted as well. Humankind, especially the now modern, young fair skinned races, and the young of any race too at times,' he chuckled,' hate to look closely at the details of a religious trend or movement. Even more than that, they dislike stepping back far enough to see clearly how the choices made in the past affect the present as well as the future for generations to come. They just want to run off with whatever idea of things is in their head and, if not, with whatever they were told growing up. They want to make things happen, without necessarily caring if it truly is going to make things better.'

'Still Victor, despite the confusion and mistakes, was it not mostly the young, with a little help from other generations, who made the 60's and 70's possible, and here we are today because of it?' I offered thoughtfully.

'Of course,' Victor agreed 'but there is the other side of it; for one the over-romanticizing of the past, with not enough love for the present and future. There is not enough understanding of the power of innocence and yet its vulnerability. Not to mention the holding up of the noble savage without respecting the power of their mistakes. Like the bones we dig up, without fully understanding the many ways we wound the land and rebirth the past into our future.'

'But Victor are we not doing that just simply by reincarnating here so many times over? Does that not bring the past into the future?'

'Good question and what a horrible curse that would be if simply true! But thankfully it is not so simple.'

Victor drew himself up straighter in his chair usually an indication that what he was about to say was important.

'Everything is alive – even Jesus knew that,' he continued. 'What we do here matters, and it does not just affect humans, but the earth itself and the atmosphere and dimensions around us with every living thing. If we pollute the ground with unjust death, debased sacrifices and thoughtless perversities, we create astral wounds that fester and grow into a primitive consciousness that causes us all harm. Where do you think all this depression, suicide, torture and murder is coming from? Most people do come to understand, once they are on the other side of the veil and return to try it differently. Of course, there are the exceptions, and these can be terribly damaged souls. They seem to be born to cause chaos and pain. Such souls need to be healed from both sides of the veil. We need to be bold and believe in our right to a greater awareness so we can accomplish these things. We must be willing to do this, so that we can clearly see what must be done, so we may rise to meet evil, fully educated and armed, everywhere that it shows itself. This is what we must all be willing to fight for. Saying and doing what is necessary is key here, and it is the mustard seed that moves mountains.'

'For a man who wrote a pagan column called Speak of the Devil, you sure do use a lot of Christian references,' I teased.

'I am talking to you, am I not?' Victor seemed slightly amused and annoyed at the same time. 'This makes sense to you. Does it not? You were raised Christian. You are not Hindu or Tibetan in this life. You are who you are, so I speak in ways you would best understand. Over time I will show you why Feri is the oldest religion and how we are all bound together on this world.'

Victor took a deep breath and paused, before continuing in an even tone once again.

'In his own way I think this was what Long was trying to do, because he was smart enough and sensitive enough to see what modern man had lost with the religions of the modern world. But he did not go deep enough. I think he lost patience, yet I still feel his *huna* has some value as a philosophical way of spiritual practice, especially if it allows itself to grow in wisdom. The practice needs to understand its place in the scope of things and become a bit more honest with itself. Of course, many people would disagree with me here.' He chuckled again. 'What most people the world over do not wish to realize is that almost everything in religious and spiritual practice has been gifted or borrowed, reworked or outright stolen. From the feathered capes, to the curved or tall head-dresses around the world, to many symbols and stories, even tools such as prayer beads. It has always been such a wonder to me that people cannot see this. What is so difficult to see and understand that common sense and common courtesy are the common doors to all? Why do people want to mucky it all up and cause so much confusion, pain, and guilt about it all? So much suffering...'

'I don't know Victor,' I answered and then mused, 'Perhaps, because people are always looking for excuses for whatever faith or perspective lays down the rules, and then people get sick of it and make a bunch of new laws, and then it becomes a big game of how to get around it all.'

'Ah, the ole "simplest answer is most likely right" trick.' Again, he was silent for a moment before saying sadly, 'People have no idea what a wonderful time we live in. We get to actually have more than half a chance to have a fairly decent life and not be hacked to death to satisfy some idiot's ego who is just itching for a fight, or be sacrificed to some god for no good reason, or a king making war, or to die in the next natural catastrophe. We are, and have been, so blessed yet we will lose this paradise if we don't wake up. I am not talking just countries here... We will lose this whole world and what a fine mess we will be in then.'

'What do you mean Victor?'

'People can be so foolish!' He tapped the floor with his

cane. 'They are all so wrapped up in those ten commandments that they forget that the very first commandment and gift to humanity was stewardship of this world. It is an important part of our life's purpose to keep watch over this world of ours, but she is treated like an abused wife. Billions of humanoid souls are here, with countless other souls, in animal and spiritual forms, who call this earth home. If we do ourselves in and damage this world for countless generations, are people so stupid to think there is no karma or accounting for such a slap against the face of our mother?'

Victor's hands tightened about his cane as he seemed to be trying to control all his emotions. 'If they cannot believe that, then what about that jealous and vengeful god that the Jews, Christians and Muslims have put so much store in? How will *he* treat his follower's for ruining his creation? Remember Eve? She was fashioned, newly made from Adam's rib, and up against the wiles of God's most beautiful and intelligent angel, who convinced her to pick an apple, take a bite, then give it to her husband. For that little piece of sin, all of creation was condemned to having painful births, and all humanity would suffer for untold generations, until his own son bought Eve's sin with his own blood.'

'Is this why this somehow has to do with North Africa and the answer to whatever seems to be in Hawaii?' I asked.

'Cornelia, this world is so old and has endured and survived much. I am not sure of the details yet, but what I feel down to my bones is that humanity is again battling an ancient evil and not just within itself. We'd better be ready to speak up and step up and turn the tide.'

I chose my next words carefully.

'Victor, you are so angry sometimes and at times you despair that humanity is too selfish and stupid to get it, as you say. So, this journey that the gods and you are sending me on, is this you saying you still have hope for humanity after all?'

Victor rocked in his rocking chair with an almost angelic smile tugging at the corners of his mouth. 'Cornelia, one day you too will come to fully understand this, if you continue on, both determined and blessed. It is Victor the man who becomes filled with rage and despair. And at times cynicism brings out the worst in me, though I try to temper this using humor – with mixed results.'

I could not help laughing.

He continued unfazed 'It is not Victor the human who is filled with optimism; it is Victor her bull and priest that is her warrior. He will do in her name what must be done and despairs not.'

(Readers might also like to read about the triple nature of the soul that Victor spoke about extensively in his classic work '*Etheric Anatomy*'.)

The Hawaiian Goddesses and Gods of Our Journey

Pele:

Also known as Pelehonuamea, meaning 'She who shapes the sacred land.' Pele is a goddess of the volcano, lava, and fire. She appears to us as either a beautiful young woman or a very old one. Pele is known to test people. Those who refuse her help, or who take the lava rocks, or her hair from her mountains, or who eat her berries without offering her respect and permission, invite her wrath. It is said her footsteps on the islands made them grow and blessed them with life. There are many stories as to why she came from Tahiti, so far away from Hawaii. Victor said Pele created a place for her people to come to and dance the *hula* in peace. The dance expresses the other side of her fiery temper.

The fibers of Pele's hair lying over lava rock

Cornelia Benavidez

Mai ka Lua aʻu i hele mai nei, mai Kīlauea,
Ke kui ʻia maila e nā wāhine o ka Lua ē
ʻO Puna lehua ʻula i ka papa
I ʻula i ka papa ka lehua o Puna

From the crater I've come, from Kīlauea,
The women of the caldera have strung *lei*s
The foundation of Puna is crimson,
covered in *lehua* blossoms.
Sacred is the fountain covered
with the *lehua* blossoms of Puna

Kīlauea Crater

Lono:

Lono descended from the heavens on a rainbow. He rules over cultivated foods such as *taro* root. He is said to have put the sun and moon in orbit around the earth by catching them in his great net and flinging them into the sky. Victor felt there were ties to the Aztec god of knowledge, Quetzalcoatl, who did not demand sacrifice.

Lono is one of the four gods who existed before this world. Along with Lono, there are Ku, Kane, and Kāne's twin brother. Lono was the god of peace, fertility, rainfall, music and plenty. In his honor, the great annual festival of the *Makahiki* was held. Sometimes he is referred to as Lono-makua - Lono the provider of the joy of learning.

An auction poster in 1996
Post-statue of the god Lono

A prayer to Lono can be found at the beginning of this book

Uli:

The Goddess Uli is the mother of creation. She is the most sacred deity in the ancient Hawaiian pantheon, in that she is the mother of all and because she is the power of the endless birthing of self. She is the mother of eternity and the source of all healing power. She sees all and knows all, she empowers all. Because of these attributes, she is also the mother of magic and science. Victor felt that when her gifts to her people were abused, much sorrow befell not only the Hawaiians, but all the people of the world, as the energies and foundations of this reality fell out of balance on many levels, resulting in our paradise becoming ill and we with it.

The Ulili sandpiper is one of the birds of Uli

The word *uli* is also used to refer to any deep dark color, whether it be the dark blue of the ocean, the dark leafy green of vegetation, or the deep black of the night sky. Here lies the darkness of birth and death from where Uli rises.

Ku:

He is the god of war, politics, prosperity, farming and fishing. He is also one of the gods of eternity, and the only one of the four covered by feathers. He has many names and rituals, including human sacrifice, which was not the case with the others. He was seen by some Victorian Hawaiians as similar to, or actually sometimes as, the Christian's Jehovah or Yahweh.

KU
(Photo: Labrac)

Also, called Kukaillimoku, which means 'the snatcher of lands', King Kamehameha prayed to Ku before he went out to battle and conquer all the Hawaiian Islands. Ku is said to have made the body of man and is worshiped in the morning and in the summer. Victor felt there were ties to the feathered serpent god Tepeu Q'uq'umatz of the Mayans who is a creator god.

The Ghadames Area of Libya

The ancient desert city of Ghadames lies close to the Libyan border with Algeria and Tunisia, half a world away from Hawaii. The old town is a labyrinth of tunnels and houses. The people of Ghadames lived in this city for centuries with little change. It was first heard of and recorded by the Romans in the 1st century BC, but there is archaeological evidence that the area's oasis was already well known in the ancient world for at least two thousand years, if not closer to four. Back in 1986, I could not understand how this place, formed of 95.8 percent desert, could be connected to Hawaii in any way. Libya had been inhabited by the mysterious Berber people since at least the late Bronze age. The Phoenicians had established trading posts in western Libya and from there travelled about the world.

After thinking about it and looking over some old notes, Victor had told me that the area from the Atlas Mountains all the way across to Turkey was a hotbed of human development. That this area was not the beginning, but the tail end, of long conflicts between the taller people trying to always lord it over the smaller people. This is why we have so many legends all over the world of such people. These conflicts had been happening worldwide and, according to Victor, one had to only follow language and symbol meanings on tattoos and petroglyph art to find the connections from Africa to the South Seas, Hawaii, and even to the British Isles. There have also been tall people and skulls found in Hawaii, for they too knew of the red-haired giants and the small people.

The Second World War and its aftermath brought many changes to the area around Ghadames. After a number of issues and quarrels under Italian colonialism, Libya declared its independence, at first as a constitutional monarchy. Beginning in 1946, stamps were produced for Fezzan-Ghadames by the French, but from 1949, separate issues were created for the Territories.

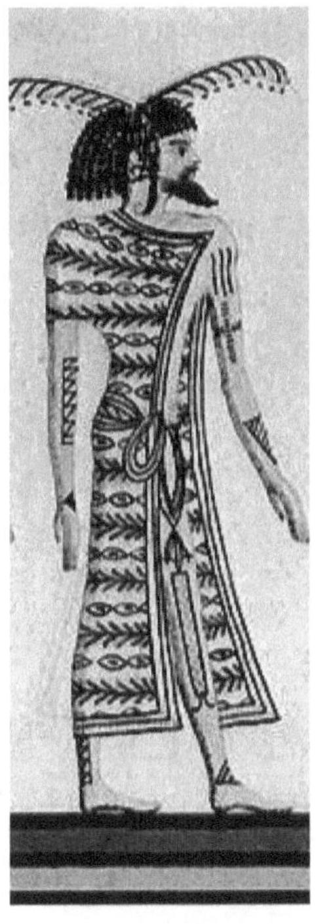

An ancient Libyan Berber person represented on the tomb of Pharaoh Seti the 1st. Unknown (original) Heinrich Menu von Minutoli (1772–1846) (drawing)

The Agazez Cross, also known as the Tuareg Cross, is a distinct design unique to the nomadic Tuareg people who populate the area. It is often found on Tuareg jewelry and is believed to offer protection from evil spirits. These beautiful stamps were used until Ghadames joined with the newly formed United Kingdom of Libya. Muammar Gaddafi, who was of the Sayf an Masr tribe, rose to power in the 1970s. After Gaddafi organized a coup against the ruling king, he also wanted to eliminate the strict social restrictions that had been imposed on women. In 1970, a law was introduced affirming equality of the sexes in the workplace, as well as fair and equal wages for women. In 1971, Gaddafi sponsored the creation of a Libyan General Women's Federation. On 25 October 1975, a law passed that criminalized the marriage of any females under the age of sixteen and ensured that a woman's consent was a prerequisite. Yet, it did not take long for him to fund terror groups around the world, though he thought of them as revolutionaries and their acts of murder as necessary.

Tuareg cross stamp

It is sad and tragic that a man who, on the one hand, seemed so progressive, turned to violence and sabotage against innocent people. Without knowing it, he threw away the chance that fate gave him, with his life ending in an horrific way in 2011.

All of the world's great spiritual teachers have taught that the middle path was and is the way of peace and wisdom. Yet, so many religions insist on extremism, no matter the cost. There is a message here, I believe, and I hope we pay attention to it for everyone's sake.

Victor grieved over the people of Africa and the Middle East. He said that we too will end up buried beneath sand and ash if we do not keep crying out for healing on a world level, and clearly stand up for the things that are sacred in life which, despite everything, still includes us.

Harmonic

I am listening for you
On the breath of the wind
I am listening for you
On the voice of a friend
I am listening
I am feeling
I am perceiving

I am longing for you
Like a lover lost
I am longing for you
Like an unsung song
I am longing
I am aching
I am painfully aware

I am watching for you
With heart-filled hope
I am watching for you
With all that I know
I am watching
I am reaching
I am seeing you there

Thank You

To Victor and Cora who stood steadfast and inspired me
To Linda for being the partner in this adventure
To Margaret and Crossroads who took in a fledging
To Norma and all those at Amron who taught me much
To John my husband who made so much possible
To my parents and sister for everything you were and are
To Marceia, I miss you every day. Love always to her girls
To Mike and his lovely family, a special Mahalo
To Bill for your support and photo help
To Mike M. for your tech help
To Diane and Sean for their extra eyes.
To Judy and Darren whose friendship means much
To all the loving and kind people of Hawaii *Mahalo*!

Also, a special thank you to Storm Constantine, Louise Coquio and everyone at Immanion Press, and to Peter Hollinghurst for his fine art on the cover.

About the Author

Cornelia Benavidez was raised in Albion Michigan by a German mother and a Mexican/American Indian and Spanish father. She grew up with a rich oral history from both sides of her family. She attended and graduated from Albion College with Major studies in Philosophy, Theater and Psychology. She lived in San Francisco for thirty years studying and working with and for various spiritual organizations including being an initiate of Victor Anderson. Also, with her husband Atty. John Doyle, she helped found H.E.A.R Hearing, Education and Awareness for Rockers. Also, she managed to sing with various bands in many of San Francisco's best venues.

Recent Titles from Megalithica Books

Coming Forth by Day by Storm Constantine

This book explores the myths of Ancient Egyptian gods and goddesses – showing how their stories relate to aspects of our lives, hopes and aspirations, and how we can learn from these ancient narratives. Through 28 deep and evocative pathworkings and rituals, the author provides a rich and vivid system of magic that the practitioner – whether experienced or a novice – can utilise in the search for self-knowledge, and to help themselves, others and the world around them. ISBN: 978-1-912241-11-8 Price: £12.99, $16.99

SHE: Primal Meetings with the Dark Goddess by Storm Constantine & Andrew Collins

The Dark Goddess is unpredictable, dispassionate, cruel, and often deadly. She reflects our deepest desires, fears, hopes and expectations. In this fully-illustrated book, Storm Constantine and Andrew Collins have selected a fascinating range of 34 goddesses, including some who are not so well-known. The pathworkings to meet them and explore their realms will offer insight into these often-misunderstood deities. (This title is also available as a limited edition, numbered hardback.) ISBN: 978-1-912241-06-4 Price: £12.99, $18.99

My First Book of Magic by Dolores Ashcroft-Nowicki

I want to tell you how the Pagan Way works, what it does, and how it makes you feel. I want you to know the joy this oldest of all traditions can bring you. The way of sharing it with humans, elementals, sprites, animals, plants, trees, and of course other pagans. *If you have a child in your life that has the look of far memory in their eyes, gift them with this guide. If you remember the child you were, read this book and reopen the gates of your wonder."* – Ivo Dominguez Jr., author of 'Keys to Perception'.

ISBN: 978-1-912241-10-1 Price: £10.99, $15.99

immanion-press.com

Immanion Press

Fiction books that may be of interest to those interested in the magical, the spiritual and the occult.

More details on our web site
immanion-press.com